Vic

MW01236171

Word of God, another man Waters But God gives the 'increase'. I hear the Spirit of the Lord saying He is increasing the glory upon your Life which Belong to Him! Blessings, Newman Smith Victory Walker July 9, 2022

From America's Most Wanted To Heavens Most Wanted

Newman C. Smith Jr.
Victory Walker

Published by: The Triune Group, Inc.
1458 Sumter Dr. SW
Marietta, GA 30064

ISBN – **9798462950377**

Author Contact information:
Newman C. Smith Jr
PO Box 156
Bartow, Georgia 30413

Email: thevictorywalker@gmail.com

Quotations from the King James Version Bible

Contents

Testimonials About The Author

To say that the testimony of Newman Smith's life is unique would be a gross understatement. Newman himself is a unique individual who had indulged in the excessive evils of a life void of God. He chose to abandon such a life style to completely and whole heartily give himself to God in Christ Jesus. His love for God and his faith in God have been the motivating factors that have led him to walk in spiritual realms not experienced by most Christians. He is a bold witness of Christ, who is compelled to share the love and power of Christ through his divine Holy Spirit encounters, and through his preaching, praying for the sick, and expressing the love of Jesus. This book contains some of those encounters in and outside the prison walls.

Norman Wilson, Retired Air Force

I first meet Newman Smith at the church my wife and I pastor in Tennille Georgia. I knew nothing about him except my daughter had invited him to church. It was immediately obvious that he loved Jesus and was sincere in his faith, but the story I heard was incredible. It was hard to believe at first because it was so wild. I found out shortly thereafter that it was all true and is an amazing story of God's grace and goodness. I have since come to know him and love him as a dear brother in the faith. His passion for souls is awesome and his love for God is contagious. He understands victory because he lives and walks in the victory that Jesus Christ has made available to us. May his story cause you to desire the same.

Pastor Chad Waller, Legacy Church

Newman has been a friend of mine. I met him at a Bible Camp-meeting many years ago in Gatlinburg, Tennessee. He has taught me very much about standing on God's Living Word by faith, regardless of any temporary circumstances. I have seen him go into many prisons and rehabs to teach the Word of God. Newman is truly a General in God's Army. I know that his testimony and wisdom which is in this book will encourage many to walk by faith and not by sight. Keep up the great work my brother in Christ and; my friend.

John Gooch, Madison, Mississippi

Newman has made a profound impact on the prison system where only God could intercede.

From living the life of a drug dealer to running a prison ministry, he accepted Jesus Christ in a prison cell and has never looked back. Newman has a real burden for the lost and incarcerated men. He changed his whole life style and traded a dead soul for the hope of bringing eternal life to those with a past much like his. Newman's faith in God to supply his needs is evident. His faith is based on God's unconditional love, and it has taught me a lot in the time I have known him.

Michael Turner

From the FBI Most Wanted List and also on America's Most Wanted Television to becoming God's man of the hour! Once a drug addict, drug dealer and living a gangster life style with many alias names, in and out of jails and prisons, serving many years incarcerated in Federal and State prisons. This is a must read of a life of sin and crime of smuggling drugs but the greatest of all the life changing power of God bringing Newman (a New Man) to his knees. I have known Newman only for a few short years and during this time I have known him as a man walking and living The Word, full of the Holy Spirit power, displaying his ministry gifts with teaching, preaching and demonstrations of the miracle working power of the Holy Spirit. He believes the Word of God and demonstrates it in his ministry gifts and calling. Newman goes back into prisons to minister the life changing Gospel of Christ, once incarcerated himself now he goes back into prisons as a prison missionary an ambassador of Christ. There are more people outside prisons walls than inside. Be set free by the power of God, even so Lord Jesus come! God will use your past as a pathway to where He called you to be!

Joyce Williamson, Minister and Author.

Acknowledgements

First and foremost, I would like to thank my God through the Lord Jesus Christ and Savior who saved me from myself and because of His mercy and grace shown to me by keeping me alive when my sin nature was full blown in the wickedness of darkness being in the fullness of rebellion and criminal intent. I could have been killed at any time but God kept me alive for His purposes for He knows our ending from the beginning. I had to repent and turn to God through Christ. God knew that I would turn to Him at the lowest period of my life and I bottomed out in my life as I was serving time in many Federal Prisons and State prisons. I also have been in many county jails all over the country. I thank God through my Lord Jesus Christ for saving me from a life of destruction. I thank the Father of Glory for bringing me into an inheritance which is imperishable, so I am full of joy unspeakable and full of glory. God through His grace has adopted me as a son into His family, all through my acceptance of the Lord Jesus Christ, and through the shed blood of Jesus Christ on the Cross at Calvary and the power of the Holy Spirit who regenerated and renewed my human spirit. I became a new creation in Christ old things passed away and I became a New Man in Christ for the Glory of God. I have received an inheritance incorruptible, and undefiled, and that fadeth not away, reserved in heaven for me. Amen! I thank God and acknowledge God so that now the change has come and I walk in His blessing and God who trained me and taught me by the Holy Spirit to be an ambassador of Christ representing the Kingdom of Heaven on earth. Now, I minister as a prison missionary I go into many prisons and in all kind of rehabs and Churches setting captives free who are snared by the devil. I am God's own workmanship created in Christ Jesus as I walk out this new life given to me in Christ. I am thankful to God for redeeming me for His glory in Christ Jesus.

1 Peter 1:3-5 (KJV)

3 Blessed *be* the God and Father of our Lord
Jesus Christ, which according to his abundant
mercy hath begotten us again unto a lively
hope by the resurrection of Jesus Christ from
the dead, 4 To an inheritance incorruptible, and
undefiled, and that fadeth not away, reserved in
heaven for you, 5 Who are kept by the power
of God through faith unto salvation ready to be
revealed in the last time.

I would like to acknowledge that I am deeply grateful to my friends Ronnie and Joyce Williamson, who are my precious brother and sister in Christ, who with their book writing skills have helped me so much by putting my chapter writings together into book format. Ronnie and Joyce are ministers for the Kingdom of God with their ministry, The Rapha Center International, Inc. Joyce is an author of many books and I appreciate their skills and acknowledge the capacity of their wisdom for writing, editing and putting her books together for publishing, so that I can draw for the wells of their knowledge in putting together my testimony book, "Victory Walker". They are a great team ministering with integrity and wisdom which God has so plainly given to them. Joyce helped me so much with editing and with her husband Ronnie took the chapters I have written and made it into a book format for the publisher. I thank God for their witness of the power of God operating in their lives. Thank you both so much and God bless you both a thousand times more. In Jesus name. Amen.

I would like to thank the Georgia Department of Correction for allowing me to take their training so I could go into their prisons to minister the gospel of Christ. I am able to give my testimony at many State prisons of how at one time I was actually one of the incarcerated, until the grace of God through the Lord Jesus Christ touched my life. All of this happened by encounters I had with the Lord while I was serving Federal time and State incarceration sentences. I am able to be a witness to those who are incarcerated that God in Christ can really change a man's life from the inside out.

I would like to acknowledge and thank Prison Fellowship Ministries, who help me in a delicate transitional period of my life. The brothers in Christ who attended a PF weekly were excited to see Elva and Gene Black the facilitators of the PF Team at the prison while I was incarcerated doing Federal time in Leavenworth, Kansas . I transferred to Atlanta, Georgia to finish out my sentence, and there was a Prison Fellowship meeting there too.

Then later on as I served a State sentence in a Georgia State Prison at Forsyth, Georgia I encountered a Ministry Team from Bill Glass Ministries “Behind the Walls”. This encounter while I was incarcerated made a powerful impact upon my life, and after I was released over the years I have been a volunteer team member with Bill Glass Ministries “Behind the Walls”. I have been a Team Member with this wonderful caring Prison Ministry at least seventeen events in various Georgia State Prisons and County Jails as of this writing. I will be attending many more prison events to come with Bill Glass Ministries “Behind the Walls”.

I also want thank and acknowledge Full Gospel Businessman's Fellowship in America who has been involved for many years with Prison Ministry. I have been going into prisons many years with FGBMFA with members Robert Cook and David Turner of the Augusta, Georgia Chapter. I received my first prison training to receive my badge with the Georgia Department of Corrections at Jackson, Georgia with the help of a group of FGBMFA ministers who were in training at the same time. For many years I have attended the FGBMFA Georgia Men's Advance at Rock Eagle, Georgia where I have met and come to know many others from the Full Gospel Businessman's Fellowship in America organization. They have assisted me in my walk with Christ and I thank God for their acquaintance and ministry as brothers in Christ.

FOREWORD

My name is Newman Smith and I am from the State of Georgia. I was incarcerated in different prisons four different times, one time under an alias name where I managed to stay under the radar in prison. I also served three sentences under my name. I smuggled marijuana and sold it most of my life unless I was in prison on a State or Federal government imposed vacation.

My first federal indictment in 1978 was in the Northern District of Georgia for three thousand pounds of Marijuana and 99 Ar-15 rifles. I was sentenced and sent to a Federal Correctional Institute in Lexington Kentucky, which was a drug rehab prison. Then upon my release in December 1982 I had no desire to change, and I would return to a life of crime. In 1984 I was returned to the Federal Penitentiary in Atlanta, then I was sentenced on the new charges later in 1984 where I was assigned to the Federal Prison in Leavenworth Kansas for a seven year sentence, plus five more years running concurrently.

I knew that I would be in a while and I started

to read my Bible, and going to the Prison Chapel because I knew that I needed a drastic change in my life, and that I could receive a life sentence if I ever came back on Federal charges again.

With the help of a prison guard, he called himself "Shotgun", while I was in the USP United States Penitentiary in Atlanta, Georgia, I was incarcerated in the AWB cell house of which he was in charge at night. I started to talk with him about the Bible truths. Shotgun had chosen me to stay out of my cell to clean up at night because everyone else was on lock-down. I had the run of the place at night and he would let me use the phone after I mopped and waxed the concrete floors, and we would talk about Jesus Christ for he was a great man of God.

After I was sentenced, the time came for me to leave the Atlanta USP and I was in transit to Leavenworth Kansas. So being in holdover status I was transported from one Federal Correctional Institution to another Federal Correctional Institution. I had decided to give my life to Jesus Christ at the USP in Atlanta and wouldn't you know the first stop was at the FCI Talladega Alabama. I was placed in a prison cell with a Christian man from North Carolina who was Holy Spirit filled. We talked about Jesus and one day he said to me, God was speaking to him and that God wanted to fill me with the Holy Spirit. I didn't really understand for I knew nothing of the gifts of the Spirit. I only knew I was saved.

He taught me from the Bible about the Holy Spirit, for my new friend was the first man that ever told me God was talking to him directly about me receiving the Holy Spirit and being endued with power for the manifestation of gifts of the Spirit. We prayed for me to receive the power of the Holy Spirit with a manifestation of the gift of speaking in tongues, after we prayed he said to me don't you hear any words coming up out of your spirit. I looked at him and said, "Hey man, I was raised in a certain family denomination that didn't teach this truth for I heard no words coming up to me out of my spirit man". He said lets pray again because God had spoken to him and said I was to receive the power of the Holy Spirit, so we prayed again and in my natural mind I was thinking the same words, "Hey man I don't' hear nothing" and I was about to say the same words again and the presence of the Holy Spirit fell on me and I begin to speak with other tongues. It kind of startled me at the beginning because I felt the presence and power of God the Holy Spirit move upon me for the first time in my life, I felt the tangible presence of God the Holy Spirit. I was wanting to say something to him about this encounter but all I wanted to do was keep praying in the spirit my new Heavenly language.

I had been endued with power from on high and received a fluent Heavenly language at that moment in time and it flowed out of me like rivers of living water. It was the powerful and wonderful presence of the manifestation of the gift of tongues given to me by the Holy Spirit. I knew I would never be the same again.

Well, after many months being transported in chains to different FCI's I finally arrived at the Federal Prison in Leavenworth Kansas. While at Leavenworth I became involved with the Prison Fellowship Ministries which came in each week to the prison, and for the two years I was incarcerated there I attended weekly meetings. After serving two years of my time in Leavenworth I received a transfer to the Federal Prison in Atlanta, Georgia, so I could get frequent visits from my family.

Leavenworth Kansas was too far from my home state of Georgia for regular visits. I was released in 1989 after almost five years on that sentence. Upon my release from Federal Prison in Atlanta I had completed approximately seven years federal time during the two times I was incarcerated in Federal Prisons throughout the USA.

After my release I went back to what I knew best; receiving loads of Marijuana. I went back hanging around my old friends with the same wrong life style. Then in 1992 some people tried to kill me and rip me off. I had a shootout in Atlanta metro area. I had weapons just like they had and I was firing a Tech 9 weapon, so I managed to get away from the scene, but law enforcement came because of all the gun fire. They found what they said was a little under three hundred pounds of high quality Sinsemilla Marijuana. Anyway, because of the drug related ambush I was posted on the FBI's Most Wanted List in the Atlanta Newspaper and after a few months of being a fugitive from justice, I was placed on the TV program, America's Most Wanted.

I was captured a few days later because of

someone who I was seeing in Miami, and another place where I was hanging out in Miami, Florida. They all knew me by my aliases for I was calling myself Lee Taylor, and they turned me into the AMW program, and the FBI so I was captured a few days later. Now I was put in the Dade County Jail in downtown Miami, Florida awaiting extradition back to Georgia. I repented and cried out to God for help. We started a Bible study in the cell and everyone called our cell the Den of Iniquity, for the worst of the worst was on the 13th floor. It was not long before God gave me a night vision which I remember to this day.

In the vision I saw the ceiling melt above me and something like liquid golden light poured into my spirit, for I could see my body of flesh asleep on the bunk bed in my cell. In this vision my spirit man had come out of my body and I was standing there with my spirit man receiving this anointing from heaven. I heard a voice of what I believed to be a man calling my name Newman Smith and I said, " I am down here." The person in the vision came down the cat walk where the guards usually walked and he stood in front of me. I reached through the jail bars and laid hands on each side of his neck and when I did the same liquid golden light anointing, which was coming down from Heaven upon me and into my spirit, flowed out of my hands into him and he started to glow with the same anointing which was upon me.

The liquid golden light was a steady stream coming down upon me from above and it was coming out of my spirit man into the man standing in front of me which I had laid hands upon. I didn't understand this vision totally until many years later. During this experience I was anointed for a calling in prison ministry and rehabs. I started to pray for people in jail and they would receive the Holy Spirit.

Many years have passed, and I have had some setbacks but the victory I walk in now does not compare to the glory that shall be revealed. Now I tell people I went from America's Most Wanted to Heaven's Most Wanted. I am a part time volunteer involved with FGBMFA (Full Gospel Businessmen) and Bill Glass Ministries. I am also a volunteer for the Georgia Department of Corrections, and independently going into prisons to declaring what God has done for me. It was my serving time in many different prisons, and by the grace of God I came to know Jesus Christ as Lord and Savior and the deliverer from my past life. I love prison ministry and the greatness of the salvation of Jesus Christ. So I continue to go into prisons whenever I can, and this book will go in prisons with me and wherever the Lord sends Victory Walker to tell my story of the power of redemption.

Newman Smith

Chapter One
Georgia Grown Country Raised

My name is Newman Smith, Jr. and I was born in Georgia and raised on a country farm. We lived close to the train tracks and at night you could hear the cry of the train called the "Nancy Hank." Sometimes my mother would say there goes the Nancy Hank as the train would be traveling from Atlanta to Savannah, and with the house windows open on sweltering summer nights you could hear the train blowing a loud distinct sound as it approached the junction on our dirt road.

We had an old push button blue fan in the living room window and during the long summer nights my dad would change the old fan to exhaust mode, that way the air would pull from the outside fresh air through our bed rooms. We usually slept under a sheet during the summer nights or no sheet at all, but during the winter we slept under a lot of homemade quilts, and we could blow a breath out and see the cold vapor coming from our mouths if we went to the bathroom at night.

My dad was born in 1919 and that's the way he

grew; up getting up early and making fires in the mornings before his brothers and sisters got out of bed. My dad didn't believe in running any heat at night, but by 5:00 am he would arise for work at Fulgums Industries and light the fire.

I was young when we lived on a rural route dirt road and that same dirt road became very slick during and right after a hard rain. You see we have a lot of red clay here in the State of Georgia and the dirt road I lived on had a couple of solid red clay hills which were steep and became treacherous during rain storms. We lived in the edge of the county and my relatives lived across the creek where we would visit them and we would travel those slick hills.

My daddy would drive us to a little white country church with tall, and I mean tall Georgia pine trees out front of the church. Every Sunday whether rain or shine, we were not going to miss going to that small community Baptist Church named after the last name of some of our kinfolks. We had wooden tables out front and sometimes we would have Sunday country dinners, in which all my relatives would cook food and bring to the church, so we could all eat and have fellowship together.

We listened to a fire and brimstone preacher who seemed to preach on going to hell every Sunday, or that's the way I remember his sermons. I could feel the fire of Hell licking up the back of my legs because of the heat of the message, and we could never forget the movies that they would show from time to time. The movies someone had made just especially to show what would happen to a person that didn't receive Jesus as Lord and Savior. In the movies the unbelievers went to a fiery furnace.

Sometime in order to make it to church in the old 1955 Ford, four door automobile that my dad owned, he would have to make adjustments. It had back doors that would malfunction and the doors would open on their own automatically because door locks were broken. My dad being innovative would take a rope and tie the door handles from one back door to the other one. My dad didn't want the doors to open and all of us fall out of the car and roll down in a ditch on one of those red clay hills.

He looked after us very well as children and we had plenty of work to do around our farm. On the rainy days the rain on the clay hills that we traveled across and also the creek we crossed to visit our relatives were treacherous. We would come up those Georgia red clay hills sideways during the rains. Sometime it was so slick we would slide into the ditch and get stuck and could not get out.

My dad would walk home and get our tractor, which happened to be an old Farmall A, which was a hand cranked tractor; no starter. We were the starter with that old hand crank, and if you didn't place your hand on the crank correctly it could kick back on you. It was so strong it could break your arm, so we had to be careful when we cranked that old Farmall to make sure we kept our thumb over the crank handle so it didn't kick back on you. Sometimes as you were hand cranking it would just slip out of the palm of your hand. I had to keep a good arm for all the farm chores so we had to be extra careful!

The farm work was all I knew about in those days, except when myself and my brothers and sister were in school; otherwise we were busy doing farm chores. We came home from school to work until the sun went down. We had barb wire and electric fences to hold the cows in their field, so we would take a hand bush sling and go around the electric fences to keep the weeds from shorting them out and starting a brush fire.

We raised our own hogs too and we would slop the hogs with scraps and water added into it. We would fatten those hogs and usually on a cold day in January, we would kill one of those huge Yorkshire hogs so we could have food on the table. My dad usually killed the hog and we would scald the hair off of the hog in an old syrup kettle cooker, while we had a hot wood fire going under the kettle, so the water would get scalding hot.

We cured our own country hams and we made our own country sausages to hang in the smoke house (which by the way never smoked) it was more of a curing house, but being country folks and we were country folks, we all called it a smoke house anyway.

We took newspapers and placed it over the wires that stretched from wall to wall. Then we hung the fresh home sausages over the wires to cure out before we would finely freeze the sausage, especially if weather turned a little warm. On the hog hams and shoulders we would rub salt over them every day for a few weeks, then we would place the meat back in a fifty-five gallon steel barrel with wooden racks. We stored it after were done rubbing and massaging the curing salt into the hog meat.

If the weather turned warm during some days during the salt curing process we would get blocks of ice to put in the barrel to keep the meat good and cold until it cured out. After the curing process was over we would place the meat in flour sacks and hang them up in the smoke house until the final curing process finished. My mother and I would go to the smoke house and cut a piece of a meat off one of the hams or shoulder after it was cured and ready to eat.

Mom would cook the pieces of ham in a black iron skillet, and the skillet was cured out the way country folks knew how. Country folk who cooked in a black iron skillet know what I am saying. My mother would fry the country ham and make red-eye gravy with eggs fresh from our chicken house, as we raised our own chickens too. We would have fresh baked homemade biscuits that only a mother's love could bake and her biscuits were the best to me.

Before we lived on the farm which my dad bought, we lived with my great aunt on the same dirt road, while my daddy and some family members were building a house to live in on the other side of the creek, a few miles away from my great aunt's house.

Growing up we had a sister who was ten years older than me and she would help my mother take care of us children. We had a real outhouse in the back yard and my sister would always get me to stand guard outside of the outhouse door because one day she had a snake crawl under the door of the outhouse while she was inside. So every time from then on I was on-guard at the outhouse door to keep the snakes away until we moved into our newly built home.

Our new house was made out of old lumber that we recycled from a house my dad had torn down. We never talked recycle talk way back then because we just gathered materials from where ever we could to build our house. We had our own indoor bathroom with a tub, commode and sink, and all installed in our new home which we moved into in 1959.

I was six year old at the time of the move and

my other two brothers and I moved into a small bedroom with one set of bunk beds and one other bed for my younger brother. That was the room where we could see the vapors from our breath because of the cold winter nights, but we were warm with plenty of homemade quilts to pull over our bodies and heads.

Our dad would have the heaters running by the time we would get up for school. I went to a small elementary school in Bartow Georgia where the first through the third grades were in the same class room. By the time I reached the third grade the small town school was closed and I would ride the school bus to begin the third grade at our new elementary school in Wadley.

I failed several grades because of poor report cards. I just didn't make good grades in elementary school so I was held back for one half of the following school year in the same grade that I had failed. I always managed to get promoted back up to the right grade at the half year mark, mostly because my folks knew the principle of Wadley elementary school and I was required to do some extra school work to get that promotion.

By the time I made it to high school I was very interested in listening to rock and roll music. My older sister and I, before she was married to a man from Augusta, used to listen to all the music she bought at record stores, or purchased at the local drug stores. When she left home with her new husband she left all her Big Bopper, Fats Domino, and Elvis records, with most of the music on forty-five's and some thirty-three speed records, along with an assortment of others teen bands which were popular around that time.

I liked music so much that I saved up enough money to buy a guitar out of a mail order catalog; maybe it was a Sears catalog. I don't remember which mail order catalog it was which I used for buying my first electric guitar, but it cost me a whole forty-five dollars.

I loved watching American Bandstand as it came on television on Saturday's. I just loved the bands and all the fancy dance moves. I was just enthralled about the whole music culture so I wanted to be a part of it myself. Then on that mail order guitar I learned how to play in opened E chord, and learned how I could play the song Wild Thing by the Trogs and a few other songs in the open chord of E .

My brother acquired a bass guitar and somehow we acquired a set of drums and we would play all of that loud noise in a back room of the house, but you could hear it all over the house. My dad had built a back room onto the house because we were getting too big for that small bedroom that the three of us lived in for a long time while we were growing up. So the band would gather in the back room to make noise.

We were three brothers and sometimes my future brother-in-law who married my younger sister would play too. He would play drums or my younger brother would play them. Every band had a name, so we were called the Psychedelic Mob. I took a can of green paint and sprayed the name Psychedelic Mob on the side of the old wooden barn. We never played together anywhere outside of that back bed room.

About the time I entered the twelfth grade in high school I transferred to a different high school in the next county over. I lacked a half unit from going into the twelfth grade in Wadley, so I could move to the next county with the grade units I had and start in the correct school year that I was supposed to be in.

When I started in 1971 in Washington County High School I went to a couple of technical school classes across town at another school. There I was able to get into an auto mechanic class for the first half of the school year, and an auto body and fender class the second half. I also found a job at the cotton mill in Tennille after school. I saved some money up and later bought a 67 Dodge Dart 273 four speed short block Mopar. I paid around fourteen hundred dollars for that beautiful car.

"1950 Ford"

Around the age of fourteen my dad was working at Fulgum Industries and my mother was off shopping for some other food items in Augusta, Georgia, although we grew most of our food. While no adults were around, my brother and I would take the extra car and go for a little joy ride. We had a 1950 Ford with a Flat Head eight cylinder motor. Sometimes we would take off and drive the field roads between the pine trees on sandy dirt roads leading through the woods to a pea field on the backside of our property.

There were other field roads on joining property next to ours and that particular dirt road in places was a lot straighter than our pea field road, so I would take the 1950 Ford Flathead straight eight and really open it up, and be driving ninety miles an hour before you could know it. Suddenly the pine trees were flying by us as I was unafraid of the danger, or I didn't even think anything about the danger at it all.

Now looking back I can see that it was really crazy what we were doing, because we could have wrecked at the high speeds we were traveling and we could have been hurt badly because we were careless. Whether I was driving or my brother driving, it was just a lot of fun to us because we were learning to drive until we could get our driver's licenses when we turned sixteen.

There also was a public dirt road that went to a place called Lewis Lake, and the dirt road was several miles long. After a few miles the dirt road came down a long steep clay hill and there was a short wooden bridge for a small overflow stream coming from the lake. The short wooden bridge had a pitch that went upward from the beginning of the bridge to the far side of the bridge leading to the dam; something like a ramp for jumping, and that's how we used it. We would be running about fifty plus miles an hour coming down that long steep clay hill and the car would jump off the bridge and we would be flying through the air and land on the dam.

The dirt road continued on the top of the dam for a few hundred feet, and the dam held the water together to form Lewis' Lake. At the end of the dam was an old gristmill, so we had to land just right on top of the dam, because on the right side was the lake and on the left side was the deep embankment of the dirt dam, and if we didn't land just right on the top of the dirt dam it could have been a disaster for us.

Our parents didn't know what we were doing but my dad knew something was not right because we stripped a few gears out of the three speed transmission a few times. Fortunately dad was a good mechanic and we would take the transmission out and replace the stripped gears with other ones. Dad would tell us not to be so rough on the old 1950 Ford, but we said nothing and just looked on and did our part to help him repair it. We learned a lot about working on cars and old Farmall tractors by helping him around the farm.

Hunting Wild Game and Camping

While growing up and living on a farm we always went hunting whenever we had some spare time. We would hunt wild game of all types, quail, squirrels, deer, and raccoon. We hunted with shotguns and sometimes we would carry a rifle if we were hunting deer.

A friend of ours had two coon dogs, one named Jack and the other one a Blue Tick hound dog named Blue. My old friend whose name was Glover would hunt coon's at night and most of the time we would go with him. Glover knew how to really work those hound dogs, and they would go ahead of us until they "treed" a raccoon. Then if the dogs cooled down from their barking, Glover would make a call to the dogs and they would always start back to barking at the raccoon that was up in the tree. We fought our way through the thick branches and briers in the woods to where the coon was up a tree with the dogs howling at the base of the tree, which was the great purpose of their training.

We were young teens back then and my brother and I had part time jobs on Saturday in a small town named Bartow. On the certain days we would camp out overnight and we would get our friend to buy beer for us at the county line liquor store because we lived in a dry county. We could ride with Glover to the Emanuel County line especially if we were coon hunting and camping out overnight down by the Williamson Swamp Creek.

Sometimes we would fish all night and burn tires for light, and sometimes we would sleep in an old army pup tent if we got tried, or we wanted to sleep off the effects of some of the beers we were consuming. We thought it was cool to be sneaky and drink like adults for at that time of life we were between the ages of fourteen and sixteen.

Nancy Hank Train Ride

Sometimes during the summer we would travel with our church family, which was mostly made up of relatives and cousins, a short distance from our home to a train station in Wadley. We all would board the train named the Nancy Hank and ride it to Tennille, Georgia where we would have other relatives and church folks picking us up at the Tennille train station. We would go to the Dairy Lane in Sandersville for an ice cream treat before we would go back to our homes. This would become a great memory for me until some years later.

I would ride the same train by myself to Atlanta, Georgia and my dad's sister Aunt Lorena Ford would meet me at the Atlanta Train Terminal and she would make sure that I transferred to the right train that was going to New Orleans, Louisiana. I would travel to New Orleans by myself to spend the summer with my older sister and brother-in-law. I did stay with them two different summers between school years, and on one occasion while I was traveling on a train to New Orleans, they met an Army Soldier traveling in the same railroad car that I was in.

My Aunt Lorena asked him to watch over me, which he did as he was traveling back to his Army Base in the New Orleans area. The soldier had a bag of fresh cherries with him in which he shared with me, and that was the first time that I ever had tasted real fresh cherries and I remember they were really good. The soldier had been traveling from his home State of Pennsylvania. I would be met at the train terminal in New Orleans by my sister Joyce and her husband John.

Chapter Two
Train Wreck

Early one morning I woke up early to eat breakfast because that day I was going deer hunting. I was still living at my mama and daddy's house where I had been raised as I had recently graduated high school. About one mile from the house were the railroad tracks, where every night we could hear the sound of the Nancy Hank blowing its horn at the railroad crossing. The Nancy Hank was a passenger train traveling between Atlanta and Savannah, Georgia, and there were many other freight trains traveling back and forth between these cities.

I finished my breakfast quickly for I was going deer hunting. I was fresh out of high school, the class of 1971. I walked outside and got in my car that was a 1967 Dodge Dart GT 273 Cubic inch with a Hurst four speed shift on the floor. It was my dream car with a lot of power and it would burn and squeal the tires going through the gears. My Dodge Mopar was a fast machine and I was living fast and driving fast and being a wild teenager who thought I was bullet proof.

I drove out the driveway with the image in my mind of a big deer, a buck with a huge rack. It was still very dark for I wanted to be in my deer stand before day light. There was a thick fog that morning, very dark and thick I could barely see the front end of my car. I drove out of the driveway onto the country gravel road in the direction of my deer stand. This deer stand I had set up several days before and I was getting excited about seeing the activity around my stand.

As I approached the bottom of Coleman's Hill the railroad tracks were somewhere in front of me. I slowed down trying to see where the tracks were, and I knew the tracks were somewhere in front of me. The fog was very thick and it was still dark, and Williamson Swamp Creek was close to the bottom of Coleman's hill whose steam added to the density of the morning fog.

LORD SAVE ME

I thought I saw where the railroad tracks were, and shifted my Dodge GT into second gear to cross the tracks. I looked intensely to find where the railroad tracks were and all of a sudden out of nowhere the black tanker cars appeared. They came out of the fog in the darkness of the night before daylight would appear. I tried to turn a sharp right to miss the train and headed for the ditch or thought I did anyway.

Suddenly I was being eaten alive in my car like giant jaws of death. The first thoughts in my mind were, I am a dead man but I did not speak out those thoughts, instead I chose another thought and said out loud "Lord save me". All of a sudden it was like some giant foot had moved my car from under the train to the outside, but the driver's side of my car was now still being hit by what I thought was the bottom outside edge of the tankers and box cars.

I was still under the steering wheel, the train was traveling in the direction toward Savannah and I was pointed north into the train with the driver side still taking a pounding. I could actually see the side of the box car crushing through the post that holds the top onto the car at the front windshield. I was being moved and shaken around in my car by the impact, like something out of a horror movie. Then the impact stopped and all calmed down except for the sound of the train that had just passed by and the hissing sound of my car engine shooting out water and steam from the damage of the train impact.

Somehow during the last of the impact I had managed to get the passenger door open, as I was trying to get out before I was dragged father down the tracks. All of a sudden the train passed and stopped the crushing of my car. What a relief that was I had survived without a scratch on my body!

Now getting out through the passenger door that I had opened early trying to escape this horror, I picked up my daddy's shot gun and ran about one mile back to my house. My daddy was getting ready for work, and I ran into the house and into the kitchen where my mama was cooking breakfast for him. I said to them "I just hit the train" my dad got up from the table along with my brother Charles and out the door we went in his car down to the railroad tracks .

When we arrived at the tracks my car was now sitting side ways in the road and blocking the road as we looked at my crushed and very damaged car, I knew it was a total loss. A

Georgia State trooper was already there on the scene and we all got out of the car and we approached each other. The State Patrol said to us, "Do you know whose car this belongs to?" My dad said to the trooper "It's my son's car." The trooper said, "We are looking for his body up and down the railroad tracks right now, and my dad replied to the trooper, "This is him right here". The State Trooper could hardly believe his eyes after he had observed the damage to my car. I had run all the way under the train because my car had disconnected the last nine cars. The train was backing up the tracks to connect the nine lost railroad cars.

Now that I am believer in Jesus Christ and the Word of God, I can look back and say through God's mercy and grace I was delivered, because of and through the prayers of the saints that had been praying for me to get right with God. I also believe that since the words of your mouth are important and I had said the right words "Lord save me," God sent an angel to deliver me in that split second between life and death. I was not prepared to meet my Maker when the train wreck occurred. The book of Psalms Chapter 91:11-12 says "For He shall give His angels charge over you to keep you in all your ways. They shall bear you up in their hands, lest you dash your foot against a stone."

In my case this time my stone was a train wreck, delivered by the power of God's love and the ministry of angels for it is also written in Hebrews 1:14, "Are they [angels] not ministering spirits sent forth to minister for them who shall be heirs of salvation?"

High School Graduation

My senior year of high School I started experimenting with drugs, especially marijuana, but I soon was turned on to MDA. Anyway my high school graduation was 971. I was smoking a lot of marijuana and I increased by smoking more and more with my friends as the new year came in. I worked at the Cotton Mill in Tennille, Georgia during my senior year of high school, and my cousin and I worked together after school on the evening shift. I would come home late at night after work and get up early to finish my high school year so I could get my High School diploma.

Somehow I managed to get by that year on a little bit of sleep. I left the cotton mill and went to work at J. P. Stevens in Louisville. I knew all the pot heads in the plant and during our breaks, especially supper we would take a ride away from the plant and smoke pot together. We would get so wasted and come back to work that way.

One friend of mine had made a homemade pot smoking pipe from a oxygen mask like hospitals use to this day. He put a pipe bowl at the end of the plastic tube and it fit nicely so we could breathe through the mask, and place the head gear on and just get wasted. After our supper, both our eyes were beaming red from smoking pot but no seemed to ever noticed. No one ever said one thing to us, so we went back and ran our machines no matter whether we were working in wet finish or dry finish at the mill. We were manufacturing cloth on our job like normal people did, but we were high on the job.

1967 Dodge Dart GT Wrecked

Chapter Three
West Texas Wreck

One cold winter morning in 1973, it had snowed the previous day and there was snow on the banks in West Texas on Interstate 20. We were close to city of Monahans, Texas, and the Interstate seemed to be clear of all of the snow, and the sun was shining. I was traveling with a man who I had meet in Fort Worth that previous Christmas at a friend's fathers house. My new friend was an older man and I was going to be twenty years old that year. We will call him Dick, and this man was a unique person to me because he could speak fluent Spanish. Dick and I were on our way to some town in West Texas to find an old connection of his to buy marijuana, but we decided to go on to Mexico instead. We would look up his friend at another time. We were Mexico bound!

Dick told me that he had been smoking pot since he was eleven years old with the migrant workers in the cotton fields of West Texas on the family farm. He was around sixty-five and I was on my last year of being a teenager. I was young and impressible and he told me along the way how he use to smuggle marijuana from Mexico in the 1950's. Dick would tell me in those days he had a hole in the fender well of some car where he could stick his hand up high and pack the fender full of pot.

We were smoking pot together and every now and then he would pull out a bottle of Old Grand Dad Whiskey and take a nip. The conversations were rich with the days of Dick's glory and how he would smuggle and sell pot way back then and he was going to show me how it was done. I was excited about learning how to smuggle pot, so I could take it back to Georgia to sell.

We were traveling on Interstate I-20, and in those days the speed limit was eighty or eighty-five mph. I was driving very fast when I hit a spot of black ice and started to skid sideways off the paved part into the medium. The 1973 Toyota Celica sports car which I had bought in Augusta, Georgia started to flip and roll down the inside medium as we were traveling west on the interstate. After rolling and flipping over in the car several times we finally stopped. Now we were sitting upright on the opposite side of I-20 in the east bound lane.

The top of the car was partially caved in on us

and I had blood running down the side of my head. I looked at Dick and asked him if he was alive and alright? Dick said that he was alive but his side was hurting him. My car was a totaled out wreck and the Texas State Troopers were arriving at the scene of the accident. The State Trooper looked at us and called for an ambulance.

We were both taken to the hospital in Monahans. My head had to be sewn up by the doctors and was full of stitches. Dick had some broken ribs but we were alive. The doctors said that I needed to be in the hospital for observation for a few days, so they rolled me out of the emergency room after sewing my head up, and wrapping my friends ribs up. They put me into a hospital room for recovery and Dick sat in a lay back chair for resting in the hospital room beside me for the first night.

Immediately we started to plot how we were going to walk out of the hospital and get a Greyhound bus ticket back to Fort Worth, in order to get Dick's station wagon. We needed to finish the purpose of our trip, and we were determined to travel to Mexico. The next day I went to the closet where my street clothes were, and we walked out of the hospital without being released by any doctor.

We went to the bus station and bought tickets for Forth Worth. It was snowing very hard as we traveled east on I-20 toward the big city. I had bought the tickets from a large stash of money I had hidden in my socks. I had been concerned the previous day of the emergency room staff seeing all of the cash which I had on me while in the emergency room.

Somehow I had managed to sneak my cash by the doctors and nurses in the emergency room, but it was over now and we were out of there without paying any hospital bill. You see for some reason I didn't have any insurance on my car for I had let it expire. You could get away with a lot of things back in those days which you cannot get away with now.

My car was a total loss and I was going to have to finish paying the $3517.00 dollars off at the Bank of Wadley, for loan. That's all a new 1973 Toyota Celica cost back in those days. My father had cosigned for the loan at the bank and I was going to have to pay it off, because I had no choice now! I was already planning to have plenty of money anyway, because I could travel to Mexico and back to Georgia with the

Marijuana from the beautiful mountains of Mexico.

Was rolled three or four times and was caved in on the top. But God spared both of us. This is a before photo.

Chapter Four
Arrested in Mexico

During the early 1970's, a friend of mine decided to go down to Mexico with me. On a trip into Mexico we went over to Boy's Town (red light district) to find our Mexican connection. Our Mexican connection liked to hang out in the place where all the women were, so we could always find him there or a certain girlfriend of his would always find him for us if he was not there.

We were always making arrangements with him to buy marijuana and if we didn't drive it across the border ourselves we would make arrangements for him to bring it to the Rio Grande River for us. We had to pay more money per kilo to pick up at the river. What we would do is wait on the America side of the Rio for him, and pretend we were fishing the river. He would show up and get in a fishing boat there that had a rope already tied from one side of the river to the other. The marijuana would be in feed sacks and he put all of it in the boat and crossed over to us. We would pay him and load it into our car for the trip north away from the border.

On one of these particular trips to Mexico we went into Boy's Town to find our Mexican connection and he was somewhere else, so we waited in his girlfriend small apartment because she lived there in boy's town. We had rolled our last joint that we had with us to smoke and we cleaned the seeds out in a small cooking pot.

As we proceeded to get high in her apartment there, and had just finished smoking all of it when there was a knock on the small apartment door, and the lady went to see who was there. The Mexican Police just happened to be walking by, or we were being set up, one or the other but I never did figure out what happened. The Mexican Police smelled the smoke from the last joint we smoked and since they could speak no English they would try to talk to us in Spanish, but we could not understand them.

The police started to look around the room to find some marijuana and looked extensively talking in Spanish to the woman in the apartment. She was pretty smart and had taken the cooking pot with the seeds from the marijuana we had smoked and poured a bag of sunflower seeds over them and was eating them while the Mexican police looked some more. She even offered the police some of the sunflower seeds and she had extended the cooking pot toward them more than one time.

The police never looked into that container holding both kinds of seeds, marijuana and sunflower. They found nothing in the apartment but just happened to overlook the container. I suppose they wanted us to pay them so we were arrested and loaded into a very old panel wagon, about a 1950's model for transport to the Ojinaja, Mexico Jail. We at least we were hoping that was where we were going.

Now as we were being loaded into this panel wagon, we saw it was fitted with wooden seats on each side for us to sit on. These seats were of rough wood on the inside of this police vehicle, and there was barbed wire instead of iron bars to hold us in. We couldn't believe what was happening to us at that time, and we couldn't even begin to know where we were being taken. We knew about the tales of brutal torture at the hands of Mexican Policeman, and hoped that was not this.

The long ride seamed even longer with our butts bouncing up and down on the dirt roads and the paved road had huge pot holes in them. It was a rough ride as my friend and I looked at each other and wondered where we were going, because we couldn't understand what the two Mexican policemen were saying to each other.

We arrived at the Ojinaja Jail and were escorted inside and seated outside a large prison cell full of rough looking Mexican prisoners. They were all looking at us Americans. We noticed right away there were no toilets, only a hole in the floor.

We waited for some time and in comes a high ranking Federal Mexican Army official who could speak English. The conversation went about why we were there in Mexico? What were we doing in Boy's Town? Then they asked how much money we had on us. I had only forty dollars left on me. My friend had nothing on him that I knew of anyway. The Mexican Army officer said to pay the forty dollars, twenty for each of us and we could go. I paid the money.

We were escorted outside to a Ojinaja police car and another Mexican policeman was driving my car. We drove toward the border in the police car. The policeman driving us told me in Spanish that I was loco as he kept pointing his finger at me. Loco was one of the few Spanish words that I knew and I knew he was calling me crazy and yes, looking back now at what happened back then, I was loco.

We arrived at the Mexico–USA. Border on the Mexican side and were let out of the police car, and the policeman driving my car got out. We got into my car and drove across the border to the American side; the good old USA! We were some happy people to be back in the USA after that encounter with the Mexican Police, and the official from the Federal Mexican Army.

On the way down to Mexico I had hide a sack of money beside a road sign on the American side because I knew better than take that kind of money into Mexico. After we had gone through the U.S. Custom's on the American side, we stopped on our way north and picked the sack of money up. On that particular day we headed away from the border; we had escaped! We knew that a worst thing could have happened to us than pay forty dollars to the Mexican's. Now we were back in USA with our lives still intact!

Newman Smith

Chapter Five
Middle Georgia Connections

I had an older friend that was a jeweler in middle Georgia and I had been smoking marijuana him with for several years in the early 1970's. He would buy some pounds of pot that I would bring back from Mexico and help me sell marijuana in middle Georgia.

At one particular time I had about thirty-five pounds left from the last trip I made to Mexico. My friend knew some older men around middle Georgia that were old moonshiner's that only sold moonshine and they wanted to expand their business ventures and get into the marijuana business, so my jeweler friend made arrangements for us to meet for the first time in the middle of the woods, and they purchased the last thirty–five pounds that I had left from my last venture from Mexico.

There were two older men in their fifties which my jeweler friend and I went to meet out in the middle of nowhere. I was quickly introduced to them and we came to an understanding about the price for the marijuana because of the larger quantity they were purchasing from me.

These men were what some would say were the pillars of the community and owned big businesses in different towns around middle Georgia.

These men were the movers and shakers of the local legal business world in several counties around. What they were really after is me and my Mexican connections. The purchasing of my last thirty-five pounds was just to meet me, and one of them convinced me to come to his office a few days later to have another conversation with him.

What I didn't know until later was that my jeweler friend had sold me as a connection for the price of ten thousand dollars which they paid him later, after I had become involved with one man who was a huge Vidalia onion farmer, and grew other crops like tobacco, etc.. Out of the two older men who met me that day in the woods, I never saw but one of them anymore and that was this onion farmer; both men were super wealthy.

At the time of this writing they have long since passed away from the earth. The man I never saw again was a well know business man with stores named by his name and as I said, I never laid eyes on him again.

I knew big money was behind all of this and they were there to bring me in. I was already getting into the wealth of this illegal source of finances and I didn't really need my new farmer friend to be a part of, or get involved with the Mexico source. I could have brought the loads back and sold them to him, but being very young as I was in my early twenties, I let the onion farmer talk me into this new partnership.

He was doing all the financing of the next load and furnished me with a car to drive for the trip back to Mexico. I was making a smaller portion of money on the profits but was going to purchase one hundred kilos of marijuana, and that's about two-hundred and twenty American pounds. On this trip, and up until this time I was always bringing back less than fifty pounds. This was a huge step up in quantity and the farmer wanted the whole marijuana load brought back to him in Middle Georgia.

The farmer sent another older man who was a large pecan farmer with me. Later on I discovered it was my connections which they were after, but they had to have me first to find the Mexican connection. My main connection was living in Ojinaja, Mexico. Many years later they would write a book about this very dangerous man who was my friend, and he died in a shootout many years later with the Mexican Army.

Before all that happened, as usual I would drive out to Boy's Town and tell one of the ladies that lived there that I wished to see him. It would not be very long before he would show up. I was there with my friend Dick from Texas and he could speak Spanish very fluently, so Dick would arrange everything where we were to pick up the marijuana.

This time because we were purchasing a 100 kilos, we needed to pick up the marijuana on the American side of the Rio Grande River. Dick and I had, on a previous load of pot found the Rancher who owned the land on the US side of the Rio. We asked him if we could go fishing from his side of the river. The Rancher had given us permission to fish the Rio Grande River. We would take out our fishing rods and fish the Rio while awaiting for the Mexican connection with the load of marijuana. There was a rope tied to two mesquite bushes, one in

Mexico and one huge bush on the American side, and also a flat bottom boat there to come across the river.

You could tell it was a well-worn path on the banks of the Rio, and this way was used very often for crossing back and forth on the river. The pecan farmer who was with us observed all of this for the first time. The pecan farmer from Georgia seemed highly nervous waiting for our connections to come over the river with the marijuana. Dick was a professional smuggler and I was learning quickly from the master smuggler himself, and for some reason I never had any fear of what we're doing.

I was obliviously trusting Dick and being young I was ignorant of the dangers of having all that cash, and the possibility of penalties which could occur if we had been caught in the act of smuggling this load of marijuana.

Finally, the Mexican connection came with the 100 kilos. He loaded all the sacks of marijuana into the boat that was on the bank on the Mexico side, and used the rope tied to the American side to pull himself over with the load. We had a pair of hanging scales like a farmer or rancher would use to weigh feed, and we weighed each sack as we loaded it into the trunk of the car, which I was to drive myself.

The weight was correct so we paid the Mexican Connection and he quickly went back into the boat and he pulled himself back over to Mexico, where there were other Mexicans waiting on him. Either they were the owners of that load or people that helped him bring the marijuana to us. They were off into the darkness of night just as we were.

We had to stop a several gates to open and close before we came to the main highway. Now I was on the main Highway following the lead car with Dick and the Georgia pecan farmer in it as we travel away from the border of Mexico, and I had done this several times before but this was the first time we were in two cars. Dick's car had a Texas license plate and a Georgia licenses plate was on the car I was driving. We both had driven for a while all through the mountains of the Big Bend National Park and out into a long straight road outside the Big Bend. It was still dark and as I approached a certain point of the road I saw car with a blue light flashing and a road block for me to stop.

It was a Border Patrol Car, so I tried to act normal. I had the window rolled down and a man with a Border Patrol uniform came up to the car window and asked me if I was an American citizen. I told him yes I was, then he asked me where I was coming from and I told him that I had been fishing on such and such man's ranch. I named the ranchers name and he shined his flash light into the back seat of my car. There he saw fishing rods in the back part of the car and he told me to go ahead.

The lead car with Dick driving had started to put on his brake lights to see if I was going to make it through that check point. They had slowed down so much that it could have alerted the officer that we were traveling together. I thought to myself that they should not be doing this, and in doing so I could have been busted with the 100 kilos of marijuana. The Border Patrolman had seen the fishing rods so my story fit and he let me go, having no idea that my trunk was so full of marijuana that the bumper was close to the ground. I use to tell people and laugh about it later that my bumper was dragging the pavement. Just a joke but it was close to the ground, but anyway, I had made it through that check point because my story looked like it was straight; that's country talk for the truth.

We went to a hotel by Interstate 20 early that morning because we had been up most of the night on the border of Mexico, and the US. Now we were pretty much safe because back in the seventies if you were pulled over by the law, they would not open your trunk. So after a little sleep we were on the road to Georgia and Uncle Dick had stopped in Fort Worth where he lived.

Everywhere Dick and I had gone previously, people thought he was my Granddaddy or Dad for no one knew back in those days. He was a Granddaddy alright for Dick was always sipping on a bottle of Old Granddad Whiskey. In State of Texas I was still too young to enter a bar by myself. The age was twenty-one to enter a bar back then, but I would often go to bars with Dick and he would tell them at the door I was his son. It was legal in Texas since I was over eighteen to enter a bar with your dad.

I just loved that old man and all we did together. A few times in the beginning Dick came back to Georgia with me. It was not long after another encounter with the Border

Patrol my friend Dick wanted out. He wanted a payout fee for the connections I had met, and we paid him. He then moved to Albuquerque New Mexico and opened up a bar. We use to talk some on the phone but I never saw the old man again and shortly after we went our own ways he passed away from catching pneumonia. The master smuggler was gone but he had taught me many things, such as how to become a master smuggler, and the things which I learned from Dick would later on cost me many years in Federal Prisons and State Prisons.

Chapter Six
Jacksonville Experience

After many years of traveling back and forth from Atlanta Georgia to Jacksonville Florida, I was being sought by the Feds for different indictments in the Northern District of Georgia and the Southern District of Texas. I had a driver take me where I needed to go. We were traveling to Jacksonville in a Smokey Bandit beautiful black Firebird with the gold eagle emblem covering the hood of the car. The car was exactly like the Firebird driven by Burt Reynolds in that movie with Jackie Gleason. You see someone in Atlanta owed me some big money, so I just took the Firebird for my payment.

We arrived at Jacksonville Beach, and we were drawing a lot of attention from movie goers that knew a similar black Firebird car was driven by Burt in that movie. I went to a beach club to hang out waiting for some friends and my driver didn't want to stay, so he drove the Firebird, and rode on the beach. Back in those days you could drive a car on Jax Beach , and even park on the beach if you wanted too. My driver decided to show off and did a spin out of the wheels showing off the car, but he did it right in front of the beach police. He was pulled over, and because we didn't have the proper paperwork for the car, because I had taken the Firebird from someone in Atlanta, the beach police hauled him off to jail. I was hoping to get the proper paperwork when I returned to Atlanta, but now the whole story has changed.

I had stayed out all night with a friend of mine. I didn't know my driver was in jail, and the beach police had found the motel key on the driver, and were waiting on me to return to the hotel. They were really looking for me, but who they captured at the motel room was me with another identification on me and it was not followed up on.

So I was in Jacksonville Florida, Circa 1978 in the wrong place at the wrong time. I was arrested at Jacksonville Beach at a motel. I had a Halliburton brief case with drugs and lots of cash in it. I ready don't know how I got away with using an alias name in that case but I did. I was taken to the Jax Beach City Jail and later transported to the Duval County Jail. The Duval County Jail was like most jails I had been in, and it was the pits.

I had been in many jails and bonded out before the authorities knew I was using other aliases, and never came back for court, but this time I would not bond out. I stayed in the Duval County Jail and they never discovered that there were federal warrants out for the real me. Remember I am under an alias name at this time, and back then we were fingerprinted on fingerprint cards done manually and not with a computer like law enforcement does these days.

I had Federal warrants out for me in the Northern District of Georgia and the Southern District of Texas, when I was captured in 1980, and that's when I served time in many Federal Prisons that I will write about in other chapters.

So as I stayed in the downtown Duval County Jail. We could have clothes and shoes brought and dropped off and the jailers would bring them to us at our cells. I would have people bring clothes and shoes to me that had the heels of the shoe taken off and drilled out so drugs could be put in the shoes, then the heels would be placed in the proper place to look normal. We were smuggle drugs into the county jail so I could still keep getting high while I awaited my court date.

Some of the people in jail with me were the bullies of the cell block. One huge guy would go to the food shoot where food was given to us like animals in a cage, and take as many milks or orange juices that he wanted, and people would have to go without because they were scared of this monster of a guy.

I saw what was going on the first day I was in the Jacksonville, Duval County Jail. I made sure I was one at the front of the line so I could get my ration of one orange juice or milk. Nobody was going to catch me in any weakness I would fight to get mine. One day I was a little late getting to the food shoot, which was handed to us through a small door in the wall, just big enough for the food trays. That day I didn't get one so I went over to the cell bully and took my orange juice that he had taken. We said a few words to each other and that's all that happened that day, but I could tell he didn't like me showing him up by taking my juice back from him. What he didn't know is that I had made a shank out of a sharp pork chop bone which was served a few days earlier.

A shank is a homemade sharp knife made any way you could use it. I made the shank in case I needed to defend myself by stabbing somebody; anybody that would challenge me. Most of the time I was doing drugs in the jail cell and I was a little crazy in my thinking back then.

A little later this bully became my friend in the cell block. We had a truce between each other because he knew he could not take my ration of food. The other weak people would have to do without their rations, and sometimes he would take so many that he could not use them all, and he would share what he had taken with me.

I started sharing all the drugs that I was getting in the jail with him. We would stay up all night talking, getting high, and playing cards. One night we were smoking a joint and the jailers smelled it and raided the cell block. Other deputy sheriffs were in the catwalk looking into my cell, as I heard the steel doors open I took what drugs I had and put them in the toilet to flush. One of the jailers in the catwalk saw me getting ready to flush them he screamed out to the other jailers "He is going to flush it," so they tried to hurry to my cell just in time to hear the swoosh of the toilet; it was gone that quick.

All the evidence was gone in one swoosh!

They came and tore the cell apart but could not find anything. I was safe because I didn't need another drug case while I was waiting on this drug case to be finished.

Chapter Seven
Old Fulton County Jail, Atlanta Georgia

I had been on the run for several years from the Feds because of a 1978 indictment in the Northern District of Georgia after being arrested in Macon Georgia with a hundred pounds of marijuana in 1980. The Federal Marshalls came to the Bibb County Jail, Macon Georgia and moved me to Atlanta, Georgia for arraignment before the Federal Courts in the Richard Russell Building.

When I was brought before the courts that day I found out they were two indictments pending, not only one in the Northern District of Georgia, but two indictments all together and the other indictment in the Southern District of Corpus Christi, Texas. The Northern District of Georgia indictment was for three thousand pounds of Marijuana and ninety-nine AR-15 rifles. The Southern District of Texas indictment was for smuggling multi-tons, along with a few other charges, because I had been caught up in a conspiracy with other people from Texas. I was being held in what would be now, the old Fulton County Jail.

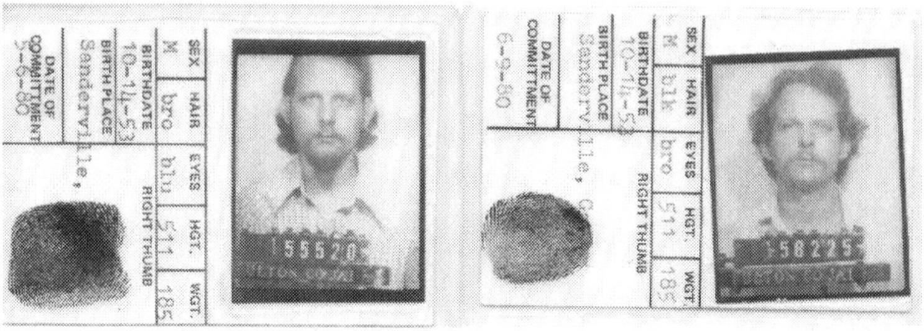

Mug shot from the Old Fulton County Jail

Chapter Eight
USP ATLANTA

In 1984 I was incarcerated for the second time at the United States Penitentiary in Atlanta Georgia awaiting sentencing, and to be transferred to a final prison destination. Let me backtrack for a moment, I already served a Federal sentence from 1980 until 1982 in different Federal Prisons, and I was paroled out of the Lexington Kentucky FCI to finish that sentence in a half-way house called Dismas House on West Peachtree Street Atlanta Georgia.

While I was in the Lexington FCI I went to church sometimes but all for the wrong reasons, because on Sunday all those who attended church were first to the chow line. I was not very concerned with understanding the real reason for going to church was to have a relationship with Jesus Christ. I was released from Lexington to the Dismas House in Atlanta Georgia on December 24, 1982. I was taken downtown to the Bus Station in Lexington Kentucky and given a bus ticket to Atlanta Georgia.

All of my life was one big drug party, and to supply my cocaine habit and going to bars; I needed more than an income from the job which I had while I was in the Atlanta Dismas House awaiting release back to society. I maxed out my sentence so I had no parole left. I was wide open to returning to my same life style as before, and I did just that.

I went back to bringing marijuana in from Mexico to Georgia until I was indicted once again in the Northern District of Georgia and the Southern District of Texas all Federal charges. Except this time I had purchased the pot with counterfeit money so I was arrested by the Secret Service in Atlanta while I was selling $100,000 in counterfeit dollars to one of my conncctions. This time I was set up because he had agreed to set me up, and I was arrested by the U. S. Secret Service for passing some of the counterfeit twenty dollar bills.

I was back in federal custody for the second time and it didn't look to good for me. This time with two federal indictments in two Federal Districts Courts. I was in holdover status behind the walls of the "USP" United States Penitentiary in Atlanta Georgia awaiting trial. I was facing a lot of time so I got my lawyer to seek a plea bargain for both cases in the same courtroom through a rule 35. This is where you plead guilty in one federal court for both charges.

I had been sentenced in the Southern District of Texas many years before, and I knew I didn't need to go before that particular Federal Judge. Sentencing day was approaching in the U.S. Court Northern District and I was to plead guilty to counterfeiting charges. I didn't know how much time I would be getting, but I decided I would take my chances in Atlanta, Georgia at the Richard Russel Federal Building.

That day I was sentenced to seven years for the Georgia case and five years for the Texas case, and before I could think about it, I just received a thirteen year sentence. The judge ran both sentences concurrent so the Judge in my case took both sentences and placed them together which meant that the seven year sentence over rides the five.

Back at the Atlanta USP I was reading my Bible and praying as best I knew how. The night guard let me stay out at night and mop, clean, and wax the hallway floors of the AWB cell house. He was a Christian and we would get into the Bible study together because everyone else was in lock down in their cells for the night. I didn't really understand until later how much God was in the middle of my situation, and as I look back now I can see God gave me favor with the guard to stay out of my cell until midnight. He would also let me have access to the phone room for extra phone time at night.

Some of the nights the guard and I would talk about the Word of God for hours at a time. I knew I needed a change in my life because this prison life was getting old, and now I have seven more years to serve. I had determined to get to know God through Jesus Christ being the door to the Father. I knew some kind of change was happening to me this time, and I suppose you could say this is where I was truly born again, and made Jesus the Savior and Lord of my life. I started going to the USP Chapel on Wednesdays and Sundays for the prison services. We would gather in the chapel and other inmates from different cell houses throughout the penitentiary came to the services too.

I enjoyed going to the chapel and having

services but this time something was different. I did not know much about fellowship with God and with other believers. I was seeking more knowledge and understanding of God in the best way that I could, and while I was in their custody it was to attend Chapel services.

I was beginning to feel a peace which I had never experienced before in my life. I know now that a spiritual transformation and renewing of my mind was taking place, but at this time I was a just a babe in Christ. I had been born again, so I was moving forward with this new life in Christ Jesus, and I found a great peace was happening on the inside of me. A change was coming and a bigger one in the near future.

I was being transformed into the image of God's Dear Son, Jesus Christ who gave his life a ransom for all who will accept the Cross at Calvary. It's a spiritual transformation for the inner man as I had become God's own workmanship created in Christ Jesus because I had received a new nature.

While I was at the USP I discovered there was a large Cuban population incarcerated because of the Muriel boat lift which President Jimmy

Carter allowed to come to the USA. Castro allowed these people to leave Cuba, and he took the opportunity to empty all of the prisons and mental institutions on the island, or that's what I was told and the media was saying it too. Anyway the Cubans filled up certain cell houses and at one time I was in one of these cell houses before I was sentenced and moved to AWB Cell house. I was there awaiting to be transferred by the BOP Bureau of Prisons and assigned a prison destination to finish my sentence.

The noise in C Cell House was almost unbearable because the noise was twenty four hours nonstop, and I was in a very small cell on one of the floors in this noisy cell house. They would set thing like toilet paper and blankcts on fire as a protest of being in prison. They all seem to know sign language so above the noise they could communicate across the void to the other cell houses on the opposite side with hand signals. After a while I was moved to AWB cell house just in time for in the other cell houses the Cuban's were rioting and were loose in the cell houses and burning anything up that would burn. The television cameras were outside the walls filming from the McDonough Blvd. Entrance to the USP, and reporting all of the goings on and I was watching on television all the reporting outside, but I was inside behind the walls of the USP.

The Cubans were climbing up on to the bars of the front windows of the USP Atlanta and setting blankets on fire and waving them at the media outside through the bars, and we were also watching all this inside AWB Cell house on television. Sometimes we could smell tear gas blown by the wind coming over into our cell house. We could see what the Television cameras couldn't see.

They were taking over the yard outside AWB and the guard would say they can’t come in on us because he had the only key. I still got a little nervous about being in the USP which seemed to be partly under Cuban control, but it was not long before everything was under control again. I had just experienced a real prison riot from the inside of the USP Atlanta.

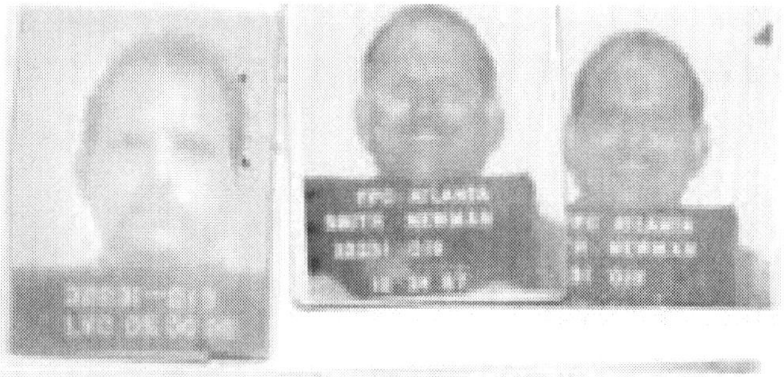

USPLK
INMATE DRIVER'S PERMIT
NEWMAN SMITH
32231-019
This inmate is authorized to drive
TRUCK
GOOD ONLY ON THE RESERVATION

GOOD FOR
ONE PHOTO ONLY
U.S.P.
Leavenworth Kansas
(Not Redeemable)

Chapter Nine
Atlanta Federal Prison Camp

I arrived from LVC a Federal Prison Camp at Leavenworth, Kansas to the Atlanta Airport, and I did exactly as I was told. I arrived at the Atlanta Camp before the furlough time had expired. We passed the walls of the United States Penitentiary where I had been incarcerated years before and I was glad I was not going back in that place.

Years earlier I was behind the walls in the midst of all the trouble they were experiencing from the Muriel Cubans. I had nothing against Muriel Cubans and they had nothing against us American prisoners for all of us were federal prisoners incarcerated at that particular time in the USP . It was just good to be back in my home State of Georgia for now as I was closer to my family so they could visit me.

While at Leavenworth, Kansas in the Federal Prison, at LVC I went to the parole board and was told that I would have to serve sixty months or five years before a parole date. A lot of inmates were getting out in one third of their sentences but I just assumed I was having to do five years straight because of the charges that I had pled guilty to and this was my second federal incarceration.

I was assigned a bed at the Atlanta Camp. They were open dormitories with shoulder high cement block cubicles with two men to a cubical. My new roommate turned out to be a marijuana smuggler from North Carolina. We had a lot in common and we would tell each other what we called war stories from our past because both of us came from the same type of background. We both were international smugglers and that was the root of our down fall, and the reason we were serving Federal time instead of a state sentences.

I was allowed to transfer my seniority where I had worked in Leavenworth to the Atlanta camp from the same prison industry named Unicor, which was all over the federal prison system. I workcd at Unicor making mailbags for United States Post Office. We made the blue hand bags carried by the postal service with the white eagle on it. I chose to work in the prison industry because I could earn some money for commissary. I was being paid around two hundred dollars a month because of keeping my seniority from working Unicor at Leavenworth which was transferred with me to Unicor at the Atlanta prison camp.

At first, I was manufacturing mail bags, and then I was promoted to quality control at the Unicor mattress division. At Unicor mattress quality control I had a great job. I had my own desk and a partner to work with which was a Cuban from Miami Florida. All the Cubans and the other inmates called him by his nick name EL Mundo. He was in prison for cocaine and El Mundo was the man, his nick name meant that he was the man that controlled the world in that business.

El Mundo and I became very good friends because both of us had been in prison for many years and still had a lot of years left to finish. At the prison law library I filed the same rule for a sentence reduction for El Mundo and he received a few months off his sentence. We used to joke about the high price lawyers, which he had paid to help him with a sentence reduction, but nothing ever happened for him through the lawyers. I went to college for two years with Mercer University Atlanta.

The professors from Mercer Atlanta came to

the prison every afternoon, and the courses pertained to the core curriculum as I was working toward a Human Resources Degree. I went to Mercer University at the camp and I was either on the Dean's List, or the Academic Honor Roll every quarter for two years. Also I spent a lot of spare time at the prison law library where I was always looking up ways to get a reduction for my sentence.

I discovered I could file a certain legal law rule with the U.S. Parole Board because of my achievements for going to college at the camp's classroom. I worked on these legal papers until I knew that it would be satisfactory for the parole board. I sent this legal rule which I found in the law library books to them, because I was filing this rulc along with copies of all my letters from being on the Dean's List or Academic Honor Roll due to my high grade scores.

For my high achievements I received letters from Atlanta Mercer University Dean's office. I attached copies of all the letters along with the legal briefs. I put it all together and it looked like a professional lawyers work. I was proud of filing my legal brief all on my own.

Now I didn't hear from the U.S. Parole Board for several months, but one afternoon at mail call I finally received my answer after two years going to Mercer University in the late afternoons and early nights, and during the day I worked at Unicor.

Now with the Dean's letters of congratulations for my accomplishments they did exactly what I had hoped for by me filing that special rule. I was granted a four month sentence reduction and I was thrilled about it. It was an answer to prayer, for by this time I had been in over four years. I received a new parole date, and I was going to be released to a half-way house in Atlanta called the Dismas House four months sooner because of my sentence reduction .

While at the Atlanta camp I was involved with several different Christian Bible studies, but the one I liked the best was Prison Fellowship Ministries started by Charles "Chuck" Colson and headed up by local volunteers. It was the same type of Christian Fellowship which I attended weekly while at Leavenworth. The volunteers would come to the Camp and hold the meetings for Prison Fellowship Ministries.

The Prison Chaplain who I knew while doing

time in Leavenworth transferred to be the new Chaplin at Atlanta USP and Camp. I was glad to see him for he was a man of God and really cared about the inmates who were really interested in the Lord. One day the Chaplain Mabry came to me in private and told me that Prison Fellowship Ministries was wanting two inmates from the Atlanta Camp to be furloughed for a two week trip to Washington D.C. for their 61st Discipleship Seminar. The Chaplin said that I was one of the inmates which he was going to recommend to receive the furlough.

Needless to say I was thrilled about being given the opportunity to go to Washington D.C. with another brother there at the camp, and we traveled there together. The day came for us to leave so we were taken to the Atlanta Airport for our flight to Washington D.C., which was like a dream vacation from prison. Two weeks, and I mean a full two weeks, Hallelujah!

So in Washington D.C. we were picked up at the Ronald Reagan Airport by staff members of this great prison ministry. We were taken to Prison Fellowship Ministry Headquarters in Reston, Virginia and briefed about the two weeks ahead of us. We arrived at P.F. Headquarters and we discovered that there were four other inmates from two other Federal Prisons there to join us for those two wonderful weeks of furlough freedom. The staff told us we were going to stay at the Adirondack Park on the Potomac River, and they had rented cabins for our two week stay.

The weather was cold and it had snowed but it was a beautiful place to stay. We all were dressed for warmth, and the staff would come pick us up at the cabins early each morning for the ride into Reston for the meetings and training at the P.F. Headquarters. We were taught by some of the best Christian teachers in America, and each day we learned more about how to present to men in prison the Gospel of Christ once we returned back to our perspective prison.

At the P. F. Headquarters we would have a different Bible teacher every few days. They also video recorded each of our testimonies on one particular day while we were there. One day we were taken to a local High School to speak to the students about some of our lives and encourage them not to follow the road each one of us had taken to end up in prison.

At the high school in the Washington D.C. area all the students came to the auditorium for us to tell them our testimonies. We made up this game some of you may remember from the TV show "What's My Line;" we made up a show titled "What's My Crime." The students would be given clues to our crimes and would be asked to match the crime with the person. I can say it was a little funny and fun.

Another day we went to the Federal Bureau of Prisons Headquarters in Washington D. C. for a visit with the head of the Bureau and it was a nice friendly visit. These men were in charge of the whole Federal Prison system population throughout the USA. We were asked questions about how things could be better during our incarceration, and just a lot of different prison questions. The big day came when all of us were going to the National Prayer Breakfast at the Hilton hosted by Chuck Colson and Billy Graham.

We met Chuck and Billy in the hallway for pictures together and Billy Graham prayed a group prayer for us. I thought to myself that here I am a federal inmate serving time and God in His mercy and grace sent me all the way to Washington D.C. to meet the best ministers in America. Not only that but we were to eat at a table with a room full of multi-millionaires.

I was seated at the table with Rose Tortina of frozen food company and the man from Chicago that started Service Masters, a carpet cleaning company. The banquet room was huge and full of people and Chuck and Billy were walking around the room talking with the quests seated at each table. We knew that all these people were major contributors and supporters of Prison Fellowship Ministry.

There were only two of us allowed to give our testimony at the National Prayer Breakfast. I can say that was one day that I will never forget. I know the Lord meant for me to be there and to experience it all. I have thought of this day quite often. At the end of the first weekend in D. C. a volunteer family came and took me into their home for Friday afternoon and all day Saturday. They asked me what places would I like to go see and visit while I was at their Washington D.C. home. So we spent Saturday going sightseeing to the Washington Monument and to the Vietnam Veterans Memorial. Then we finished the day at the Smithsonian Museum. What a wonderful time I had spending the weekend with this Christian family who had the love of Christ flowing from them. They were the real deal!

The next day we were back at PF Headquarters with another teacher of the Gospel of Christ. They were great men and women of God expounding and teaching us more about God and the Lord Jesus Christ. We were going to have a graduation on Saturday for the 61st Discipleship Seminar which would be our last afternoon in Washington D.C. This was going to be a special graduation for us. We were the 61st class of Prison Fellowship Ministries because this was and had been going on for years.

Chuck Colson and his wife were there for the graduation along with all the weekend sponsors that let each inmate stay at their house for that special weekend. All I can say is that we were all thrilled to be a part of Prison Fellowship Ministries and it's just something that we all will never forget.

At the time of this writing I am still in touch with one of the inmates I met there in Washington D.C., and he has a large prison ministry and is still going into prisons to minister the Gospel of Christ and the love of Jesus. My friend has done so these years since he was released from prison himself. I am also a prison missionary ministering the Gospel of Christ in Georgia State Prisons and I also speak in rehabs in Georgia and Florida. I have been involved with a ministry in Jacksonville Florida ministering to the homeless community.

Attending 61st Prison Fellowship Discipleship Seminar in Washington DC on furlough. Met with Billy Graham and Chuck Colson at the Washington DC Hilton Hotel.

Chapter Ten
Alias Names

In the seventies I used to fly out of any Airport, especially old Atlanta Hartsfield Airport, before it changed its name. I would call and make reservations in the name of the day which I was to fly under. While I was at the airport ticket counter I would say, "I have reservations in the name of so and so" then I would pay for the ticket with cash and off to the gate I would go. I would use many different alias names, and back then if you had a pocket full of cash nobody questioned me or even asked to see an ID. I used so many different names I couldn't remember them all.

Later on I had a miniature birth card from Texas that a friend had given me and one of the names on the identification was Allen. I remember the full name but that's not important right here to say it but I started using the name Allen with everyone I would meet, and in all the many ID's I would acquire over the many years. I would use the same name Allen in all future ID's so I would always have on me an ID with the name Allen on it with many other names around the name Allen. I was on the FBI list in the seventies for the first time circa 1977 and on the run from indictments from the Northern District of Georgia.

The indictments were conspiracy charges and were a list of overt acts where I had brought in three thousand pounds of Marijuana into the Atlanta area, and had purchased ninety nine AR15 rifles. I was reading the Atlanta newspaper one Sunday in one of my hideouts in the Atlanta area. I was using Atlanta as a hub for my Marijuana enterprises back in the day.

Anyway, there I was reading my real name in an article written in Atlanta newspaper about purchasing nincty nine AR15 rifles. Nothing was mentioned in the article about the three thousand pounds of Marijuana until I was captured in Macon, Georgia in March of 1980. I had a real state ID on me saying that my alias name was Rodney Allen Phillips, but it didn't do me any good for I had been set up while doing a large marijuana transaction outside of Macon Georgia at someone's country home.

The GBI and the Macon drug squad already knew who I really was at the time of the arrest, because someone had advised them of my real name before I showed them my alias ID during the arrest. Computers were not so sophisticated at that time and I could usually make a bond under any alias name, and I would be gone before they could really find out who I was, but it didn't work this time.

I had made bond on arrest charges like this many times before and was released and off into the sunset I would go to get a new name once again. So back to all the ID's! Back then I called using all these alias ID's paper tripping. I didn't use my real name until many years later but of course in Federal Prison they knew who I was and I was under my real name.

One time in another state I got busted with drugs and I had another alias name, and I was kind of trapped because that was before I learned how to paper trip with all the ID's. I would use someone's ID whom I knew. I just hired a lawyer to work a plea bargain and went to a county pea farm, or that's what it was called. All this was happening while I was on the FBI wanted list for the indictments in Atlanta area, the Northern District of Georgia.

Beside this, there were Federal indictments in

the Southern District of Corpus Christi, Texas, division of the Federal courts. I did not know about these indictments from Southern Texas until the Macon Georgia arrest in 1980. Now I was in prison under an alias name in another state serving out another drug sentence.

I was serving this drug sentence in another state under this alias of someone whom I knew, but the system did not know who I really was. I was really nervous the whole time I was at the pea farm. I thought any day the prison authorities would find out my real name. The day before I was to be released, one of the prison guards told me that my counselor wanted to see me in their office. I was thinking they had found out by this time who I really was. I was shaking in my boots nervous, walking down the hallway to his office; with lots of thoughts going through my mind.

I knocked on the door of my counselors office and he said come on in, so I walked in he said to me, "You know you are getting out tomorrow?" He asked me if I needed to call someone to pick me up. Whew! What a relief! I picked up the phone on his desk and I called a friend of mine to come pick me up the next morning.

The next morning I was released back into society, free again! My lawyer never knew my real name but the police had confiscated a lot of cash which I had on me at the time of my arrest. Back then there were no laws on the books where they could keep your money, so the lawyer got all my cash back from the police. I had enough money to pay the lawyer and the lawyer gave me a cash reserve in escrow upon my release. I went to the lawyer's office and received my money out of the escrow account that he was keeping for me.

Free Again

Remember the Feds are still looking for me but I am free again and it's time for another alias name. There were some lady friends of mine who knew who I was. They would do all the research for me at the local library. They searched to find a name of someone that died around my age. Then armed with all the new information, off I would go again with my new alias name.

In some states I knew people who had access to blank birth certificates and I would make up a name which I wanted to use. We would boil tea and stain the certificate to make the document look old before I would use it. Then with this technique it would work very well, for in the seventies all you needed was a copy of a birth record to take the drivers licenses test. Someone I knew had a vacant home for me to send my new drivers licenses too. Then when the new driver's license was mailed, it was sent to the address I used on the license. Someone would pick it up and bring it to me. I had a different name for every alias I used back in those days, I called it paper tripping.

Fort Worth to Mexico (8-24-16)

I was invited to go to Texas for Christmas because I had a new 1973 Toyota car to travel there, and my friend had asked me visit his dad. We had gone to Elementary and High school together, and my friend wanted us to visit his dad who lived in Fort Worth, Texas. We were visiting for the holidays, so I said, "alright lets go." While visiting at his father's house I was smoking a lot pot during this time. As I was smoking my last joint in the bed room where I was staying, his dad came home and smelled the pot smoke and opened the bedroom door.

I thought he was going to raise his voice about smoking pot in his house but all that he said was, "He knew an old man about sixty-five who smoked marijuana since he was eleven years old." Well, I was out of reefer so I asked could I meet his friend and he said he would call him. In a short period of time an older man came and I was introduced to him. His name was Dick and I asked him if he knew where I could buy some marijuana. Dick told me he had a friend who was an American Indian who had a load of marijuana he had just received from Mexico.

We went over to his house, and I was thinking of buying a bag to smoke, but when I was told that I could get a pound for one hundred dollars, I thought to myself I have a thousand dollars on me. I will buy ten pounds and take it back to my home in Georgia to sell and make some money. You see, I had been paying around two hundred dollars a pound in Athens and Atlanta, Georgia. I was selling what we call lids of pot and depending how hard pressed the pot was, I would have a four finger or a three finger lid which was close to or one ounce of marijuana.

I sold all the pot in lid bags using flip top sandwich bags for that's what we had in the early seventies to use. I was charging twenty dollars a lid, and I had more money at one time than I had ever had before. One pound brought me a three hundred twenty dollar, and up to four hundred dollars if I made twenty lids from one pound, so it was a great return on my money. I soon ran out of marijuana to sell and I didn't want to pay the higher price by buying marijuana in Georgia.

I called Dick in Fort Worth, Texas, and my new friend told me to come on out to Texas and we would work out the details for another load of pot. By this time I wanted at least twenty pounds to take back to Georgia. I arrived in Fort Worth and was staying at Dick's house. I found out my new friend, the American Indian is waiting for another load of marijuana to arrive from Old Mexico, and it could come at any time. This was the winter of 1973-74 and I had just turned twenty years old. I was young and didn't know very much about what I was really getting myself into, because I could only see dollar signs, and in America, that's just what American's do.

We would sit around just to figure out ways to increase our bank accounts. I never cared that what I was doing was illegal, because I would justify that everyone is doing it, so I would too! After all, I was being blinded by the money and basically I was making plenty of money, and I smoked marijuana for free.

Anxiety

After being in Fort Worth, Texas for almost two weeks staying at Dick's house, our Indian hippie friend was still waiting on the load of pot to come from Old Mexico. Dick and I were tired of waiting on that load of pot and he began to tell me about getting loads of marijuana from some Mexican friends that he knew down toward the border of the Texas and Mexico.

Dick said that he had been buying marijuana from the same family since the 1930's and through the 1960's when he had lived in Pecos, Texas on his daddy's farm. On his family farm a Mexican man had let him smoke pot with him at eleven years old while working the cotton fields in West Texas. How about that, Dick had been smoking marijuana since he was eleven years old and now we were traveling to find the remnants of that family, but we were looking for an older Mexican man, if he was still alive.

We made a detour as we came close to Fort Stockton, Texas and decided we would go and cross the border into Mexico, because Dick knew some people there. We figured we would come back later to find his old friend's family if he was still alive. We were now traveling toward Presidio, Texas where we crossed the border into Mexico. After all most of the marijuana in the USA was coming out of Mexico, so we were looking for the source of our supply.

I had big dreams and money was my king at that time! I was still blind about what I was doing but I was with the master of smuggling, my friend Dick who had been buying marijuana in Mexico and towns on this side of the border since the 1930's. Dick was going to teach this young man how to smuggle marijuana across the border from Mexico to the land of opportunity, the United States of America.

We arrived in Old Mexico and were in a town called Ojinaja. We went to a place called Boys Town (red light district) where Dick found an older woman who he had known many years before. Dick could speak fluent Spanish for he had married a Mexican woman in his younger years, and was raised on a farm in West Texas where he learned to speak Spanish. Dick spoke Spanish while we were hanging out in the bars.

While there, we were waiting for someone who was connected to come talk to us about buying Marijuana. Later that day a young man showed up and Dick had a long conversation with him about our business being there. Anyway the man that came took off going somewhere and I assumed that he went to make arrangements for us to make a buy. The young man came back in a few hours and told us that the marijuana was going to cost us forty-five dollars a kilo. Needless to say I was overjoyed about the price for that was less than twenty-five dollars a pound.

The young man road in the station wagon with us out to a desert place to pick up the marijuana and pay for it. We were going to take a big chance and drive the pot back across the border. We were in Dick's 60's model Chevy Nova station wagon and there was a lot of space over the top of the gas tank to hide the pot. We still had four kilo's left to hide after all the space above the gas tank was full, so we decided to break down a spare tire and put the extra pot in there.

We broke the tire apart and placed the last kilos of marijuana in the tire, and they fit with no problem. We put the tire back together, so it would fill up with air, which turned out not be such a good idea. We went to a Mexican gas station in Ojinaja to fill the tire back up with air. I stuck the air hose to the tire valve stem and marijuana blew out of the tire all over the front of the gas station, and I mean it was blown everywhere! It was very obvious to all who saw the pot lying around what we were up to but no one said anything because of the young Mexican man that accompanied us.

There were young and old Mexicans sitting and standing around and they saw the whole thing happen. Pot was everywhere on the ground blown out of the tire edge by the air pressure, and as I looked around I just lifted up my hand at the scenario and grabbed the tire and stuck it in the right side wheel well where it came from, and then we headed for the border and made it across.

We were safe and traveling toward our destination to Fort Worth, and from there we would travel to Georgia for me to sell all the marijuana.

All I had in those days were people who I would front lids to and sell pounds by the lid (lids were less than an ounce), but now I needed some pound buyer's to buy all this load. I went to the people that I had bought pounds from when I first started, and now instead of buying from them I was wanting to sell to them. Some of them I found out could not sell all that I had, so I had to go see other people to help me get rid of all my pot.

I was still supplying some of my lid dealers with pounds to sell. Sometimes sales would bring almost four hundred dollars a pound. Remember, I paid less than twenty-five dollars for one pound in Mexico, and a kilo was 2.2 pounds or a thousand grams and I paid forty-five dollars a kilo for the marijuana in Ojinaja. I was getting around eight-hundred a kilo broken down in lids. I had purchased the marijuana by kilo weight but sold it by the pound or smaller quantity according to US measurements. I was making a profit around seven-hundred and fifty dollars on some of the kilos. Most of the single pounds I sold for around two hundred dollars each but that was still a huge profit of over four hundred a kilo, as I had only paid forty-five dollars a kilo (2.2 lbs.) for the marijuana in Mexico. Well it was not long, I was out of pot and heading back to Texas with a bigger stack of cash for a bigger load.

I arrived in Texas at Dick's house, but this time the load of marijuana was going to be so large we could not drive it across the border because there wasn't a place to hide that amount. We would have to pay extra money for the Mexican's to bring the marijuana across the Rio Grande River for us to pick up on the American side of the river.

The Rio Grande River flowed between the U.S.A. and Mexico Border. We went into Mexico to meet the source of our supply of marijuana and we made all the arrangements for the pickup, and we never paid anyone until we had the load in our trunk. We would buy a pair of Hanson hanging scales and weigh each burlap bag full of kilo's so as to not get shorted on the weight. The burlap bags were all printed in the Spanish language and seemed to be burlap feed sacks. Loaded once again, I would drive from the border to Pesos, Texas, and sometimes to Odessa before we stopped for the night to get some rest for the long drive back to

Georgia. This would go on for many years before I would be busted in Atlanta, Georgia for the first time.

Fort Stockton To Van Horn

After the last trip to Mexico and a close call of running into a late night border patrol check point; we decided that it was time to try and find the family with connections who Dick had been telling me all about. So we went to Fort Stockton, Texas, and we drove up to a house that he had described to me. It was a house who the old Mexican lived in that we were looking for.

It was said that he used to keep fifty-five gallons drums full of marijuana for people to buy. Dick had told me all about his smuggling and going to this particular house and picking whatever marijuana he was buying from a variety of different fifty-five gallon drums. To hear Dick tell the story, it sounded like the room was full of pot drums. The last time he was there was in the 1960's but this was the early 1970's and we were looking for same house in Fort Stockton, Texas.

We drove up to what Dick thinks is the house that he used to make buys of pot; and he gets out of the car. Now while I sat in the car. I saw some Mexican young people come to the door. They were speaking Spanish, so I could not understand what was being said but from my observation it looked like he was at the right place. Someone went back inside and retrieved a phone number and I saw them give Dick a piece of paper with something on it and it turned out the old Mexican man we were looking for they were his relatives, for Dick had been talking in Spanish to them. Dick came back to the car and told me how he was still alive, but now he was living in Van Horn, Texas. Now we have his new address and phone number where he lived, so we could go pay him a visit.

His relatives called their uncle who was the old Mexican connection and told him Dick was looking for him. He told us to come to Van Horn that he would be waiting on us. So off to Van Horn we went to find his old friend who we were looking for which was a safer way to buy and another Mexican connection to talk with.

We arrived in Van Horn to find his house and Dick and I got out and went to the door. An old Mexican man came to the door. He and Dick talked in Spanish and the man came out of the house. We walked around his house into the backyard to talk. Dick had told me that he had been to prison before on the Texas chain gang, and it turned out that he and this Mexican man had been on the chain gang together in the 1940's.

They both started to speak in English so I could understand everything being said, and I knew he could get us a load of marijuana with no problem. The old Mexican man was not expecting us to be carrying that much money on us because I had come with ten thousand dollars to purchase pot. He looked at me and said are you crazy? Do you know who you are riding with? He was talking about Dick and he proceeded to tell me how he and Dick used to rob people back in the day for less money than I had on me. He told me they used to tie people to trees and leave them.

All that talk still didn't scare me. Dick told him I was like the son whom he never had and we had been together for a while, and had been purchasing loads of marijuana in Mexico. I had been driving the last few car loads which we had brought from the border.

Now Dick's old connection became my new connection. The old Mexican said he would make a few calls and get things worked out for us. We talked about his cut of the money and we stayed a few days in Van Horn and then one day we all left to travel to Marathon, Texas. I knew we were going to meet someone there to make all the arrangements to pick up a car load of marijuana.

Once we arrived in Marathon we went to meet another Mexican man who I would follow to the border. We had Hanson farm scales that we had been previously using to weigh the sacks of marijuana. I was carrying the ten thousand dollars in my pocket, and the old Mexican man, Dick and I followed a pickup truck down to the border. We were in the Big Bend National Park when we got off the main road onto different dirt roads. We were eating dust like there was no tomorrow! We came to a stop and were in the mountains on a high hill and the moon was bright. The man in the pickup truck started to make some type of whistle and someone whistled back and they whistled back and forth for maybe a minute.

The man from the pickup disappeared in the bushes and came back with a mule train of horses laden with sacks of marijuana, and several other Mexicans all speaking Spanish. I would listen and pick out a few words every now and then, but Dick could speak fluent Spanish and he would tell me we were getting a hundred kilos of marijuana. That's two hundred and twenty American pounds for the ten thousand dollars which I had in my pocket.

They unloaded the horses, for the sacks of marijuana were strapped across the horse's backs like giant saddlebags. We weighed each sack of marijuana and the weight was correct and I paid them the money. We loaded the trunk of my car and about day light we started traveling north back toward Marathon.

I followed the pickup back to Marathon but the old Mexican man from Van Horn was now riding with the whistling Mexican and Dick. I was alone and listened to some AM radio station all the way from Fort Wayne, Indiana. This was the same radio station that I could pick up in Georgia and the other station was WKLS out of the windy city Chicago. Sometimes at night you could pick up these power stations from Texas to Georgia.

I stopped in Marathon to pick up Dick and the

older Mexican but the older Mexican stayed with the whistling Mexican man. Dick told me later they were all family and they would take the Uncle back to Van Horn. Dick and I were traveling toward Fort Stockton and then on to Odessa, and there we would get on I-20 East going to Georgia.

I dropped Dick off when I was going through Fort Worth, Texas and off to Georgia I came. Sometimes I would drive all the way because I was so hyped up with adrenaline for what I was doing, and then sometimes if I was sleepy I would pull over and get a hotel room. I never slept very long as I would wake up and would get back on I-20 East traveling to Georgia with the load of marijuana.

Chapter Eleven
The Shoot Out

I carried a large load of marijuana to a new stash house not knowing that I was being set up to be ripped off. This was the night that I lost an untold sum of money from a load of pot, and I almost lost my life while I was fleeing a drug-related ambush on September 13, 1992.

Some crooked people that I trusted had led me into an ambush and rip-off. I unloaded the bags of marijuana into their house into a huge freezer I purchased to keep the pot in, because the freezer would keep it fresh and free from mold. I had purchased the freezer and had it put in their house several weeks early, so when I was ready to fill it up it would be there. The marijuana was high quality Sinsemilla bricked in twenty-five to thirty pound blocks. The pot was grown in the fertile growing regions of Mexico. I was good at what I was doing and, handling the sale of very large quantities of marijuana that I went myself getting the job done.

Sometimes it only took a phone call to have the load delivered to Atlanta. I was moving so much pot that the Mexican Mafia would tell me that they didn't want to know anyone else. I suppose they felt safe working with me than others. I would always work selling pot unless I was serving prison time. Now looking back, I served seven years federal time in the 1980's and was released from the Atlanta Federal Prison in 1989. I didn't waste any time getting back in touch with the Mexican connections and started all over again until the shootout in September of 1992.

Now back to when I was leaving the stash house in the country. The house was set back off the main road, and when I walked out to the car, and arrived with my machine gun in one hand and a brief case of cash I had carried with me in the other. I had a strange feeling that something wasn't right before I walked out of that country house! When I got into the car, the car wouldn't start. Immediately I knew someone had tried to sabotage the car, and I realized very quickly that I was able to get the car started by holding the gas pedal to the floor.

I couldn't turn around so I had to go down the long drive way backward with the gas pedal held to the floor. Suddenly I began to receive bullets from the weapons of assassin's fully dressed in camouflage. I raised my weapon and like a wild man I started shooting back at the assassin's, who were meaning to take my life and rip-off my load of pot.

I blasted them through my car windows. This was like a scene out of some gangster movie. I was moving so fast backward that I jumped the ditch and onto the road. I was able to drive out of the drug related ambush with a car full of bullet holes. I was bleeding on my face from flying glass from the bullets that came in through my windshield. None of the assassin's bullet's hit their target; me! I then saw a car coming, so in order to keep from hitting the car I turned the wheel sharp and into the ditch.

After the car stopped with a huge jerk due to the steep embankment, I jumped out of the car. A man had stopped to help me because he thought it was just a car wreck. He was driving a pickup truck, and I jumped into the back of the pickup. Immediately I told him some people were shooting at me. I told him to drive me somewhere close to Interstate 85, and that we needed to move quickly before bullets would be fired at me in the back of his truck.

He took off quickly and took me out of the area. I called a friend of mine to come pick me up, and when the man dropped me off I gave him some cash for the safe ride out of my situation. When my friend arrived I jumped into his car and off we went. We made a complete get away, but because of all the noise from the shootout the neighbors had called Gwinnett County Police. They were inspecting the wreck and called a helicopter to help locate the missing driver of the car, but I was long gone by then!

About a week later my photo appeared on the FBI's Most Wanted section of the Sunday, September 27, 1992, Atlanta Journal/The Atlanta Constitution. Each week fugitives who are sought by the FBI and believed to be in the Atlanta Metro area were identified in that part of the Sunday Metro Newspaper. Now I was a hunted man and a man in hiding, until I could make arrangements to leave the Atlanta area.

Chapter Twelve
America's Most Wanted On Television

Dade County Jail Thirteenth Floor

On Wednesday January 20, 1993 I was arrested at the Omni International Hotel downtown Miami Florida. I was on the F.B.I. Most Wanted List, and in the Atlanta area they were looking high and low to find me. I left Atlanta Georgia for a safer place to stay, and I had three authentic state driver's licenses for identification with three different names. I could choose which one I wanted to use at any time.

I use to fan the id's out like a deck of cards and say, "Who do I want to be tonight?" I thought I was pretty safe because I had already been stopped by a Florida State Trooper up in Tallahassee, Florida. I gave the trooper my identification using the one that stated my name was Lee Taylor. He had stopped me on Interstate 10 for speeding while I was driving my personal limousine which was registered in another name. I had my suit on so I was looking like a limo driver who was on the way through the capital of Florida to pick up some important person.

The Trooper was very courteous to me and went to the patrol car to check my Lee Taylor ID on his computer. I checked out clean and received a speeding ticket. I purchased a money order and sent it in to pay for the ticket for the speeding, so I would not set of any alarm bells with the Lee Taylor name. I had enough pending problems with the law back in Georgia.

I was just traveling through Tallahassee, Florida on my way to Jacksonville where I rented a penthouse suite under my alias name. I had a friend in Jacksonville that knew a man who owned a penthouse suite on the top floor overlooking the pier on Jax Beach, and that's where I was staying becoming one of my new hide outs. I rented the condo under the same name and introduced myself around town when it was necessary as Lee Taylor, but most of the time I used a nick name so most people didn't know any name but my nick name.

I had a friend who lived in Jacksonville Beach just a couple of blocks away from my new condo rental. I was in Federal Prison with him in Atlanta, Georgia some years earlier while both of us were serving out Federal prison sentences . It's always nice to see old friends who I had done time with, and get to know them on a different level of association.

At that time my friend Louis was talking about wanting some money to start a used car lot, nothing big just a small used car lot, so I loaned him the money. I was shopping for another personal car so we went to some car dealerships that he knew. We went together and bought a car from a dealership under my new name. I paid cash for the car, but broke up the payments because of the cash; we didn't want to set off any alarms. I paid half one day and went to a banker my friend knew and received a cashier check to pay it off the next day when I picked up the car and drove away.

I had a nice car and a nice condo overlooking the Jacksonville Beach pier. I was ready to relax because of all the heat from law enforcement around the Atlanta area. Some nights I would pull the limo out of the garage and drive it to some clubs. I am a great harmonica player and I would go to this blues club on Beach Boulevard and there I would play with some make shift band on open mic night.

Sometimes the players were well known musicians from world renown bands just getting together to have a little fun. If I mentioned the famous ones I played alongside with you would recognize their names, but this story is about me and the grace of God that was tracking me down, even in the midst of my darkness it wouldn't be long before I would be arrested in Miami, Florida.

America's Most Wanted – AMW

On a nice Monday night many months later I drove to Miami from Jacksonville Florida. I arrived on Tuesday morning, and I didn't know I had been posted on the America's Most Wanted TV program that Saturday night. I was in Miami to pick up another set of ID's with passports and all the goodies that I needed to have a long vacation somewhere over seas, but I didn't get a chance to pick up any new paperwork.

I went by a shop on Biscayne Boulevard where a man ran a Sharper Image Store in the Bay Side shops. Some months earlier I had purchased a B & O stereo from him under the name Lee Taylor. I did not know on Saturday night he happened to be watching the America's Most Wanted and saw me on the program. He must have gone and looked up the paperwork which I had filled out to purchase an expensive stereo with cash. I had also been in the store purchasing silk shirts and gadgets over the past few months while I was on the run.

When the manger saw me there that morning he started acting very different and I picked up on his vibes because he was saying some off the wall things to me. Anyway, I became very nervous and told him I would be right back, but I left and never came back.

I then went to the Omni International Hotel and checked in under the name Lee Taylor. I called a girl friend of mine and she came over to hang out. The next morning I started to get phone calls from the front desk asking me to come down to pay for another day, because I had paid with cash for one day the day before. It was very early when the front desk started calling and I knew I had at least until eleven o'clock to pay. I told them I would be down later to pay and I hung up the phone. A few minutes later they called back and said, “If I wanted to stay that night I needed to come pay for the room." I just told them I would be down in a little while when I got dressed, but it was not long before I received another call from the front desk. I got out of bed and dressed to go down stairs as it was obvious the front desk was not going to leave me alone until I came down to pay.

I stepped out on the upper floor that I was staying on and was overtaken by a special Federal Arrest Fugitive Squad that had been flown in overnight from Washington D. C. to arrest me. I had been in a drug related ambush in Atlanta, Georgia some months earlier, where I had a machine gun and was considered to be armed and extremely dangerous. All this was related to being in that shoot-out with those rip-offs that decided to kill me over three hundred pounds of high grade Sinsemilla marijuana.

When I was arrested in Miami, Florida I had three ID's in my wallet. I thought to myself why hadn't I used one of the new ones to check into this hotel, but I had grown comfortable with the name Lee Taylor. When I was booked into the Dade County Jail in Miami they found my other driver's licenses in my wallet and tried to question me about how I received authentic state issued identification but, I asked for a lawyer.

I was clean when I was arrested, because I had snorted up the small amount cocaine I had brought with me to stay awake while I drove through the night trip to Miami. I was not charged for anything in Florida, but then I was there in Miami at the Dade County Jail on Thirteenth Street. I was extradited back to Gwinnett County Georgia which was in the Atlanta Metropolitan Area. I had been indicted for trafficking in Marijuana and some other charges that were pretty serious.

While I awaited extradition to Georgia, several months had passed and my lawyers were filing motions on my behalf while still in Dade County Jail. During this time I decided to repent and get my life back on track with God. I repented in Jesus Name of being sidetracked by doing my own thing. You see I knew I had a calling upon my life and God through Jesus Christ had dealt with me for being side tracked many times before. I just wanted to go the way of the world like most people do and was chasing the dollar, and it didn't matter to me to traffic in marijuana to attain money. I had come up during the late 60's and early 70's with a drug culture all around me.

Now back to repenting before God in the power of Jesus Name. I became sincere once again with the Creator of all and a few of us started a Bible study in the cell that held about sixteen men. The authorities at the jail called the 13th floor that we were on the "Den of Iniquity," because our floor housed the worst of the worse. We would glorify God even in the midst of our circumstances, for most of the fellow jailed prisoners were not in our bible study. God was dealing strongly with a few of us in that cell.

One night I had a night vision from Heaven, and in this vision I saw myself get up out of my body. It was my spirit man and I looked back to see my body of flesh laying asleep on the bed. I was standing up by the prison bars leading to the catwalk, and I heard a man calling my name saying, "Newman Smith," and he repeated my name once again "Newman Smith", so I called out to him, "I am down here" because the voice was coming from up the catwalk where I could not see. The man came down to the cell where I was and stood there with me, and the jail bars were the only thing that separated me from the man in the vision.

About that time the concrete ceiling up above me melted and something like liquid golden light came down from Heaven upon me. I was anointed and glowing all out from my spirit man. About that time I put my hands through the bars and on each side of the man's head who had called my name, and the same liquid golden light flowed into him because he started to glow like me. The liquid golden light was still coming down upon me from Heaven for it was a steady stream, and the same liquid golden light flowed out from my hands and was transferred into him by the laying on of my hands.

There was a man named David and he was back on a motion for a new trial. David was already in the Florida State prison system for murder, but he was trying to get the life sentence overturned by getting a new trail. David had an altar beside his bed on the floor. His Bible was open to the Book of Psalms with a black rosary cross laid over it. He positioned fruit around the Bible with two containers; one with red color and the other container with water that was clear. He had all of his enemies and people like the state prosecutor, along all of the names of people from the state of Florida who had anything to do with putting him in prison with his life sentence in the red container.

Then in the container with the white clear water were all the names of people who were on his side for his freedom like David's new lawyers and his family. I had never seen anything like this before, and another cell mate Ereseler told me it was a Santeria religious ceremony something like magic, so he could get the results on his case that he wanted.

The definition of Santeria is a pantheistic Afro-Cuba religious cult developed from the beliefs and customs of the Yoruba people incorporating some elements of a religion, merging with the worship of deities, and the veneration of Roman Catholic saints. He told me that it is practiced in Cuba and elsewhere.

Anyway, the power of God though the Holy Spirit was opening the eyes of my understanding concerning spiritual gifts. These gifts are imparted by the Holy Spirit and for believers in Jesus Christ who is the Son of God, our Redeemer, for through Him Jesus Christ reconciled us back to God. The Holy

Spirit of God was changing me from glory to glory by the Spirit and through the gifts of the Holy Spirit and the gift of discerning of spirits was operating in my life.

God was teaching me something about the evil side of this ceremonial ritual who this state prisoner named David was practicing in our cell. The gifts of the Spirit are listed in first Corinthians Chapter 12: 7-11 and verse 10 says: "To another the working of miracles; to another prophecy; to another discerning of spirits; to another divers kind of tongues; to another interpretation of tongues." verse 11 says," But all these worketh that one and the selfsame Spirit, dividing to every man severally as he wills."

One day I was laying on the bottom bunk in the jail cell and I was directly across the aisle from the bottom bunk of this man. What happened next was awesome! I was looking in the direction of the altar when I had a vision. I saw a demon represented as a snake, and it was trying to hide from me, but I saw it through the gift of discerning of spirits. This is one of the many gifts of the Holy Spirit, and in the vision the demon tried to strike me, but was unsuccessful. I went and told one of my cell mates and he said to me that was his last strike. The next morning a guard told David to pack it up and that's the last time I saw him.

FBI Most Wanted Atlanta GA. Area

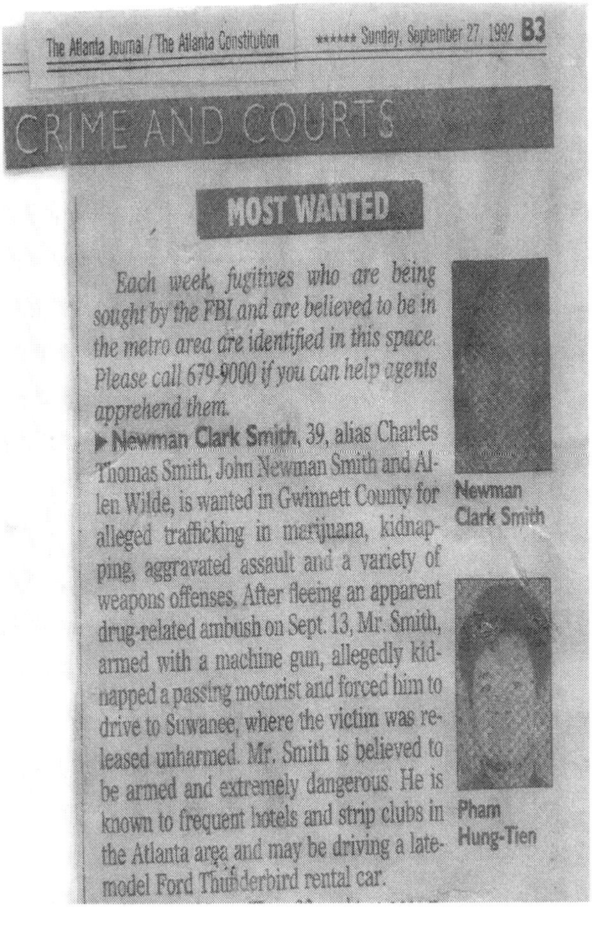

The Atlanta Journal / The Atlanta Constitution ****** Sunday, September 27, 1992 B3

CRIME AND COURTS

MOST WANTED

Each week, fugitives who are being sought by the FBI and are believed to be in the metro area are identified in this space. Please call 679-9000 if you can help agents apprehend them.

▶ **Newman Clark Smith**, 39, alias Charles Thomas Smith, John Newman Smith and Allen Wilde, is wanted in Gwinnett County for alleged trafficking in marijuana, kidnapping, aggravated assault and a variety of weapons offenses. After fleeing an apparent drug-related ambush on Sept. 13, Mr. Smith, armed with a machine gun, allegedly kidnapped a passing motorist and forced him to drive to Suwanee, where the victim was released unharmed. Mr. Smith is believed to be armed and extremely dangerous. He is known to frequent hotels and strip clubs in the Atlanta area and may be driving a late-model Ford Thunderbird rental car.

Newman Clark Smith

Pham Hung-Tien

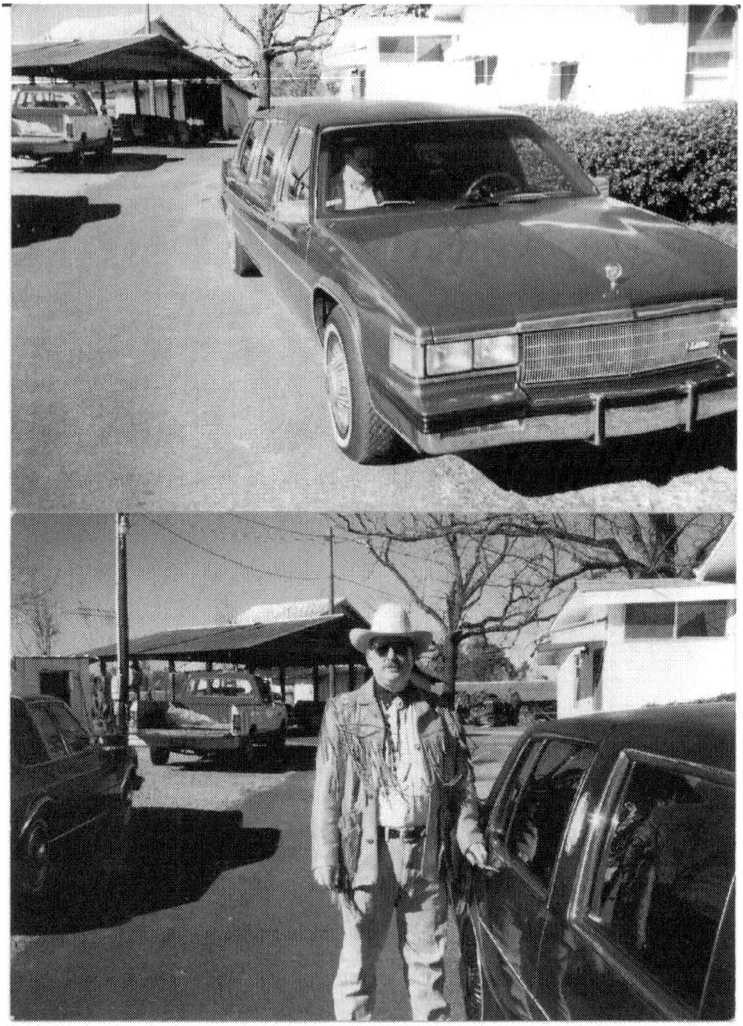

My Personal Limo's Back in the Day

Chapter Thirteen
Gwinnett County Jail

After traveling for a few days with some overnight stays at some other county jails along the route, we arrived at Lawrenceville Georgia, Gwinnett County. I was in the holding tank for about a day before being booked in as a new prisoner, then I was transferred to a cell house they called Pods. That was the first time I ever heard a cell house called a Pod. Everyone in that Pod had not been sentenced in the courts yet, so all of us were awaiting our court date.

Gwinnett County was a fairly new county jail in 1993 and I was given one of the new cells where I was glad to see it was a single cell. At night we were on lock down, but during the day time we could come out into a day room and sit around talking with the others that were in the same Pod. There were some tables in the day room and they were enough for all of us to sit down during meal time. When our meals came they were brought into the Pod so we never went out of the Pod. The only time anyone of us would leave that Pod was on the county bus headed for the Gwinnett County Court House.

I was waiting on my lawyer and the trial courts, and was to be an inmate in the Gwinnett County Jail system for one and a half years until the process was finished. I was in a single one man cell in the non-sentenced Pod for over a year before I was ever sentenced and moved to another cell house. In that new Pod were all of the people that had finished with their trial court, had been convicted and sentenced to the Georgia State Prison system. We were all awaiting our trip to the Georgia Diagnostic Center in Jackson, Georgia.

Now back to the non-sentenced pod where I was for over a year. I studied the Word of God from the King James Version of the Bible, and during this time I started to hear the voice of God very clearly. Sometimes I would only come out of my cell for chow because I was so intrigued with the message in the Bible, and it was like I had a hunger for the Word of God. The more I read the more hungry I became, and I could not be satisfied.

The guard that was assigned to our Pod was a Christian and there was a multi-purpose room in which we could have a personal bible study every day, and there were some other people who were interested that were in the Pod with me. I became the facilitator or leader of this bible study, but it really was the Holy Spirit doing all this working of putting the things together for my life. It is now obvious to me at the writing of this book that I was in training for the ministry of the Gospel of Jesus Christ. I could not learn enough fast enough to fill the hunger for more understanding of the Word of God that was coming from within my born again human spirit.

Voice From Heaven

After many months of prayer and personal bible study along with our group bible study, I walked into my single cell where I was alone. As I shut the cell door it slammed shut sounding with a loud clang because it was solid steel door with an electric lock. At that point you knew you were locked in until a guard let you back out. All of a sudden I heard a loud voice that spoke to me and I knew immediately that voice came from out of Heaven. God had spoken a personal word to me and later on I would realize that word was a rhema word or a spoken Word from God. God spoke to me loud and clear for God said to me in a powerful voice, "Clark I am going to take you to new heights in my Word".

Nobody called me by that name for that was my personal family name. Everyone in the cell house including the guards knew me by my first name and last name, Newman Smith. Wow, I looked around and saw I was in my cell alone, I look up toward the concrete ceiling. I started saying to myself that God just spoke to me out of Heaven. It was a strong voice and a voice of comfort that was building up my spiritual life more by the second. It was the voice of love.

John3:16

16 For God so loved the world, that he gave his only begotten Son, that whosoever believeth in him should not perish, but have everlasting life.

Miracles Happening

After we all started a Bible study, the group started to grow larger. I would lay hands on my new friends that were as hungry as the rest of us for the word of God. We all were hungry for more of God, and we would pray to be filled with the Holy Spirit and the Holy Spirit would come upon them and they would begin to speak with tongues like I did. Then one of the brothers came into the Bible study one day saying his girlfriend had a test done and it showed she had a lump in her breast. She had been told that they needed to take out a lump of her breast.

I told him to stand in gap for his girlfriend by proxy and we laid hands on him for her healing. When she went to have the lump removed they did some further tests and discovered the lump had disappeared. My friend had talk to her and told her we had prayed and everything was going to be alright, and that's the way it turned out. We were operating in faith. We had real faith in the living God in Jesus Name and our faith was manifesting answers to our prayers according to our faith. Our believing faith was moving the hand of God. “Glory to God.”

Access To Faith Books

There was a prison ministry from Oakhurst, Oklahoma that sent Harrison House books that were seconds to people in jails and prisons. They received those books as a donation to the prison ministry from Harrison House Publishing. I would write the prison ministry and they would send me an envelope full of books to read. I received some really great books to read and to learn how to operate in faith. I had a mini book of Charles Capps,

"God's Creative Power Will Work For You".

Mr. Capps taught about confessing the word of God over my life, and in that mini book he listed scriptures for backing your confession of the Word of God. Also about using Mark 11:23-24 and speaking to mountains, and I had one huge mountain looming in the court system of Gwinnett County, Georgia.

I was learning what real faith was because of these books, and one other book I received was a book about the prayer of petition. I had never heard of taking scriptures from the Holy Bible and writing a petition of prayer by putting the scriptures together so that you could receive an answer from Heaven. It seemed to me that the scriptures became my faith to receive answers to the prayers that I was praying.

One of the prayers that was close to my heart was a prayer for God to intervene in my case, as I had been indicted in Gwinnett County. The indictment was for trafficking in marijuana and a few other gun charges along with kidnapping. You remember that I had been in a shootout with some people that were intending to kill me for the illegal contraband. Anyway it was obvious that I was still here, and that was by the grace of God. I tell people when I testify of God's goodness in pursuing me that God sent His angels and delivered me from the mouth of the loin.

Speaking to Mountains

I would read the Charles Capps mini book and confessed the scriptures written in it almost every day for many months. I also wrote a prayer of petition with the scriptures, and with that petition I was petitioning the Courts of Heaven for mercy and grace according to the Word of God. I had done research to see how much time that I would serve because of the parole guidelines, and on certain sentences that were given out in the State Courts. Once you were sentenced and you were in prison, it was up to the Georgia Parole Board for the decision on your release date.

Anyway I petitioned God in Jesus Name that I would not receive more than ten years and I had the scriptures to back up my prayer of petition. I was speaking faith to that mountain and it happen exactly and I believed. I receive ten years to do five years in prison and five years on probation. I was learning how to operate and agree with God according to His Word. This was the beginning of speaking to mountains according to Mark 11:23-24 and I was learning how to have a wonderful fellowship with God in prayer and confessing what God said about me as a son.

I was beginning to understand that God In Christ had given us certain rights, benefits, and privileges because we accepted Jesus Christ as our Lord and Savior. Now as children of God we are citizens of Heaven and we have access to God the Father through Christ and the Holy Spirit. After a year and one half in the county jail I was sentenced and ready for the dreaded trip to Jackson, Georgia for classification, and to be sent to a Georgia State prison where I would finish my time.

Chapter Fourteen
Al Burrus State Prison

Sometime in 1994 I arrived at Al Burruss State Prison in Forsyth, Georgia, before Christmas of that year. After I arrived I was escorted to the prison cell K-22 in K House. I arrived with my mind full of the Word of God and increasing daily as I studied the Word. What a blessing it turned out to be that God had sent me to a place where I was in a single cell, so I was able to study the Word many hours a day.

One day in my cell the Holy Spirit gave me a revelation of righteousness as He open the words in Romans 5:17, and that was a beautiful moment in my life for I knew from that minute forward that I was a free man and that I didn't have to try to have a righteousness of my own before God. God had given me a revelation in my spirit and I understood that God had imparted the free gift of righteousness to me through Jesus Christ Himself and through the abundance of grace, I could walk in His righteousness as a gift and God would supply me with the power of the Holy Spirit, and make it a present reality of this revelation in my spirit.

I was accepted in the beloved Jesus Christ and that God was in Christ, reconciling the world unto himself, not imputing their trespasses unto them, and hath committed unto us the word of reconciliation. Glory to God, here I was in prison, but I was more free in prison because of this wonderful revelation. I am more free now than I was on the outside in the free world while I was doing my own thing.

Also the Word says, “For he (God) hath made Him (Jesus Christ) to be sin for us, who knew no sin, that we might be made the righteousness of God in Him.” Glory to God, for God Himself had made us the righteousness of God in Him, and He placed us believer's in Christ and has given us His righteousness. God made us righteous and we are to believe, receive, and walk it out by faith.

While I was in Al Buruss I starting having many dreams and visions from the Lord. The chaplain knew something was different about my relationship with God than the average inmate, and he use to come by my cell to talk with me. The chaplain would come and ask me, “What's God telling you.” Most Sunday's he would let me speak for ten or fifteen minutes before he would bring the message.

I was paroled in August of 1995.

Chapter Fifteen
Speaking to Mountain of Parole

This is my testimony as an inmate in the Georgia Prison system of how I spoke my parole into existence using Mark 11:23-24, and it is a demonstration of the Spirit and of the power of faith in the truth of the promises of the Living Word of God.

It takes faith and faith is your answer. It takes faith in the promises of God for the power of the Living Word to bring forth the manifestation of the wholeness of the promise. You must take a promise from the Word of God which applies to your situation and put your faith into action by speaking to your mountains. My mountain was that I was in a state prison serving time and I wanted out! Written faith without action is dead, and a living Faith speaks the desire not the problem.

"Now Faith" speaks directly to the mountain which is your desire for it to be removed and cast into the sea. Jesus Christ said to "Have faith in God". Do you believe the words of Jesus Christ? Well since you do you are on your way to removing mountains. It does not

matter what your mountain consist of. The Word of God says in 2 Corinthians 1:20 "For all the promises of God in Him are yea (YES), and in Him Amen, unto the glory of God by us."

2 Corinthians 1:20 (KJV)
20 For all the promises of God in him are yea, and in him Amen, unto the glory of God by us.

Mark 11:22-26 (KJV)
22 And Jesus answering saith unto them, Have
faith in God. 23 For verily I say unto you, That
whosoever shall say unto this mountain, Be
thou removed, and be thou cast into the sea;
and shall not doubt in his heart, but shall
believe that those things which he saith shall
come to pass; he shall have whatsoever he
saith. 24 Therefore I say unto you, What things
soever ye desire, when ye pray, believe that ye
receive them, and ye shall have them.
25 And when ye stand praying, forgive, if ye
have ought against any: that your Father also
which is in heaven may forgive you your
trespasses. 26 But if ye do not forgive, neither
will your Father which is in heaven forgive
your trespasses.

I am talking to believers here who believe that Jesus Christ was the Son of God and who believe He was Lord and Savior of the world, especially for all who accepted the work of the cross because you needed a Redeemer. Jesus Christ became our Redeemer and the perfect sacrifice while we were dead in trespasses and sin. God reconciled the world to Himself through Jesus Christ. (Read 2 Corinthians 5:17-21) We have a sin nature which is a fallen nature which separated us from God. We inherited this sin nature from the First Adam who caused the fall of man, but now God sends the Last Adam (1 Corinthians 15:45-47) Jesus Christ who became the head of a New Creation by going to the cross and shedding His precious blood for us to be redeemed. Glory to God!

When we accept the finished works of the cross God credits righteousness to our account by giving us His standing (1 Corinthians 5:21) and God assures us through faith that we are born again from above. We now have a righteous standing through the blood of Jesus Christ to approach God as a new creation man or woman who is born again from above. Now that we have been born again by accepting Jesus Christ as Lord and Savior, we walk in the newness of life. God Himself did this work for us so we are accepted in the beloved Jesus Christ our Savior. Now we are members in particular of the family of God and God becomes our Heavenly Father.

This mountain moving faith will not work for you unless you forgive all offenses. I had to forgive all the people involved which led up to my arrest. I had to release all things with a spirit of forgiveness, so that my faith could activate the promises given to me by God written in Mark 11:22-26.

A living faith activates the promises of God into your life. This is the life of faith which we were created to walk by the light of God's Living Word. We are qualified by the Father through the blood of Jesus Christ to receive a new nature, which has been restored for fellowship and relationship with the Father, so we can live this life more abundantly. God has become our supply of all things as we grow in the knowledge of Him, and He is sufficient to help us by the power of the Holy Spirit to walk out the remainder of our days with His blessings.

We can appropriate Mark 11:23-24 by

speaking to the mountains. My mountain was I wanted to be free from incarceration in a State prison cell. I don't know what your mountains are, but it works the same no matter what mountain problems you are speaking to. Now that we are born again from above through the blood of Jesus Christ we can appropriate all the promises of God.

Speaking my parole into existence
Romans 10:8 (KJV)
8 But what saith it? The word is nigh thee, even in thy mouth, and in thy heart: that is, the word of faith, which we preach;

Let's talk about the Word being near you and in your mouth and in your new heart, which is your new nature, also it is called the hidden man of the heart. The heart of man or "The spirit of man is the candle of the LORD, searching all the inward parts of the belly." [Proverbs 20:27] Now that we are born again our regenerated human spirit is the candle or the light of the Lord, so we sow the seed of the Word from Mark 11:23-24 into our hearts for it is the word of faith which we believe and speak. You see the word of faith that I preach is proclaiming something. The word "preach" means to proclaim, which means its "for claiming," and any promises in the Word of God is for claiming as your own.

You can drive the stake of faith into the exceeding great and precious promises which you are claiming as your own like Mark 11:23, by speaking to your mountain-problems. Notice that the saying or saith in verse Mark 11:23 is mentioned three times. You have something to say by speaking to your mountain-problems. I was speaking to my incarceration and saying, "Be removed and cast into the sea". I said it over and over again many times a day and then I would call myself a free man.

You see real faith is in your heart and in your mouth and faith activates the promises of God in Mark 11:23-24. I would like for you men and woman of God to understand that Jesus Christ has already given you the authority to proclaim his word. Jesus said "YOU" speak to your mountains. Just like Jesus said in said Mark 11:23 "For verily I [Jesus Christ] say unto you, That whosoever [means you] shall say unto this mountain, Be thou removed, and be thou cast into the sea; and shall not doubt in his heart, but shall believe that those things which he [means you] saith shall come to pass.

He [means you] shall have whatsoever he saith. Verse 24 Therefore I say unto you, What things soever ye desire, when ye pray, believe that ye receive them, and ye shall have them.

Template for Speaking to your Mountain-Problems
Mark 11:22-24
22. And Jesus answering saith unto them. HAVE FAITH IN GOD. 23. FOR VERILY I (JESUS) SAY UNTO YOU, THAT WHOSOEVER SHALL (SAY) UNTO THIS MOUNTAIN, BE THOU REMOVED, AND BE THOU CAST INTO THE SEA; AND SHALL NOT DOUBT IN IN HIS HEART, BUT SHALL (BELIEVE) THAT (THOSE THINGS) WHICH HE (SAITH) SHALL COME TO PASS; HE SHALL HAVE WHATSOEVER HE SAITH.
24. THEREFORE I (JESUS) SAY UNTO YOU, WHAT (THINGS) SOEVER YE (DESIRE), WHEN YE PRAY (BELIEVE) THAT YE (RECEIVE) THEM, AND YE (SHALL HAVE) THEM.

Now Father, here is what you said through Jesus, You said that I can speak to my Mountain. So I am saying to ________________ be thou and be thou cast into the sea. Now your my Mountain and I speaking to you in Jesus Name and you must obey me according to MARK 11:23. JESUS said that I can speak (BE THOU REMOVED AND CAST INTO THE SEA) and you will obey what I say, in JESUS NAME. (REPEAT OVER AND OVER) I can't begin to say how important this is to do!

You repeat this over and over until it becomes a reality in your spirit and you will know it's done! Then you keep saying over and over until the manifestation comes. Faith has a voice and it's upon your lips and mouth and in your heart. Life is in Mark 11:23-24 and the daylight of victory will dawn upon your life. Jesus said His words were Spirit and Life. The Holy Spirit may give you other things to add to this for your situation, so don't limit God. The victory belongs to you! Along the way as you are speaking to your mountain-problems, and you just thank God it's done because God watches over His word to perform it according to your faith. You believe you receive and you shall have whatsoever you say. Be sure not to quit before you reach you desired results. Glory to God!

Chapter Sixteen
Indictments Be Removed

I was a born again spirit filled believer and I left California to come back to Georgia. I was living in Dana Point, California, and I would tell people God had a sense of humor because He had sent me as far as you could go in the USA to be away from Georgia without be in the Pacific ocean.

I was released from a Georgia Correctional Institution in 1995 from the time in 1992 where I was in a gun battle with killers and thieves, that were going to steal all that pot from me. Someone wanted to kill me for all that Sinsemilla (high quality seedless pot), but I escaped during the drug related ambush. The cops came after someone in the neighborhood heard all the loud shooting and called the police. I ended up on the FBI Most Wanted List and a few months later, on the America's Most Wanted TV program. I was captured in Miami Florida the same week AMW aired.

In 2001 I left California and came back to Georgia. I went to Atlanta and started to hang out with old friends. We really did care for each other, but it was for the wrong reasons. I went back into the business in the Atlanta area until I was caught in Roswell, Georgia and indicted for trafficking in marijuana and cocaine in 2008. The case was turned over to the District Attorney in Fulton County Georgia State Court.

I am writing this chapter to teach and show you how great the mercy and grace of God is. I am going into great detail about what I have learned about Mark 11:22-24 speaking to mountains and for the people that don't know or understand, I pray that you will rise up with the words of Jesus concerning speaking directly unto mountains in your life.

Mountains are any problem, no matter how great or powerful their situation is screaming at you, don't ever give up. These mountains are speaking to you that you can't do anything about them. In the natural world these mountains may look like that you will just have to deal with it. I am telling you right now those kind of thoughts are a lie. It may be a fact but it is not the truth. The word is the real truth, and it's what the word says that matters.

You can operate in faith according to the

scriptures and speak to your mountain no matter if that mountain is it screaming at you, speaking to you, and saying that I am impossible and I will not move. That mountain of a problem is lying to you.

Jesus said in Mark 11:23-24 you can have what you say. Faith speaks to mountains and they will remove but you have to speak His words. They are the Words of Jesus. They will be the Words of your victory which is in your mouth and in your heart. The Words of Jesus are spiritual manna from Heaven. Jesus is the bread of life and His word will sustain you. Jesus said His Words were the Father's Word and He came to proclaim the beautiful Words of Heaven. So with the promises from God's Word's you can boldly come unto the Throne of Grace, and receive mercy and find grace in your time of need. The words of Jesus are spirit and life and to you and it is faith for your victory for your situation.

Hebrews 4:16 (KJV)
16 Let us therefore come boldly unto the throne of grace, that we may obtain mercy, and find grace to help in time of need.

The Word of His Grace came to deliver us and

the Word came down from Heaven to portray what the Heavenly Father is like and Jesus was the love walk of the Father in the form of a man. The walk of the God of pure love walked with Jesus Christ and he was a man just like us. He was filled with the Holy Spirit and power and went about destroying the works of the devil.

Mark 11:21-24 (KJV)
21 And Peter calling to remembrance saith
unto him, Master, behold, the fig tree which
thou cursedst is withered away. 22 And Jesus
answering saith unto them, Have faith in God.
23 For verily I say unto you, That whosoever
shall say unto this mountain, Be thou removed,
and be thou cast into the sea; and shall not
doubt in his heart, but shall believe that those
things which he saith shall come to pass; he
shall have whatsoever he saith.
24 Therefore I say unto you, What things
soever ye desire, when ye pray, believe that ye
receive them, and ye shall have them.

Now during this time I was in Fulton County Georgia County Jail for the Roswell, Georgia case. I was moved to Fulton County by the Roswell Georgia Police Department. I was called for a court hearing early one morning and when I appeared in court, the court did not have any paper work from the Roswell Police department. The Judge dismissed the case and I was released from the Fulton County Jail. I could hardly believe what had just happened. Once I was released, I called an attorney friend of mine in Atlanta. He called and the District Attorney told them I would be indicted at the next grand jury.

I waited and one day a court summons came for me to appear in Fulton County Court. I could not afford a private attorney so I was appointed a public defender. No disrespect for public defenders but we called them public pretenders. I will say it was a normal procedure for me to hire an attorney, but I was on the bottom and could hardly look up. I needed God to intervene in my behalf. I sure did need a miracle now to get out of this indictment, and this mountain was screaming at me saying, you are going back to prison for a long time.

This mountain was laughing at me and saying I am too big for you this time and all you have is a public defender. The mountain was saying you can't even afford a private lawyer Ha Ha! What you think you are going to do now? Ha Ha!

After a few court hearings I was offered a plea bargain of twenty years. Twenty years just to take a plea? I don't think so said my mind. I said to myself, I will never plead guilty to any charges of any indictment anymore, and I said I would go to trial. I had my doubts where this was going with a public defender. I could guess where this was going because I had already done over ten years in prison; seven years federal time and over three years in state institutions.

I had been before many judges over the years, and this time I had a co-defendants in this case, which I knew they would not turn on me. They were indicted for lesser charges, and we were going to trial together. They had their own public defender and I had mine.

I must also admit that my mind was a little foggy because I was on prescription medication Oxycontin for over two years. I was going to the pain clinic to get my medication because of a neck surgery. All during this time I was out of fellowship with God, but all of that was going to change soon. I was forced to move to my house in Middle Georgia. because I could not afford to stay in Atlanta anymore. So because of the 2008 Fulton County indictment, in 2009 I moved to back to my house.

I kept hearing words in my ear that I should get it over with, and just hang myself in the huge pecan trees around my home. I was spiritual enough to know where those words were coming from, even though I was severely depressed for having to come off my medication 80 mg. of Oxycontin. I was taking two a day like the bottle said but I was snorting the pills up my nose. It took me two years to get my head straight from all of those years abusing Oxycontin, and I was also snorting some cocaine along with the pills.

It was 2009 and I was back at my house with no money and no drugs. I said to myself it's time to get straight and come back in fellowship with God through Jesus Christ, which was a bright and right decision, I was like the prodigal son coming back home to my Father. I was obviously on the bottom and I started looking up to God once again. I knew I could speak to the mountains. In the past I have experienced the most awesome mountain's being removed. I was out of fellowship with God for many years and I needed God and that was the time to bring the impossible to pass and I knew how.

Being back in fellowship and relationship with God, I began speaking to the mountains according to Mark 11:23-24. I had a mountain which was an indictment hanging over my head, and I knew the power of the God I served for it is written, if God is for us who can be against us.

Mark 11:23-24 (KJV)
23 For verily I say unto you, That whosoever shall say unto this mountain, Be thou removed, and be thou cast into the sea; and shall not doubt in his heart, but shall believe that those things which he saith shall come to pass; he shall have whatsoever he saith. 24 Therefore I say unto you, What things soever ye desire, when ye pray, believe that ye receive them, and ye shall have them.

What I did was that I would hold the indictment which was my mountain in my hand and speak to it, "Be removed and cast into the sea". I am speaking to the indictment but this time I can literally hold the Fulton County indictment in my hands and speak to it over and over. I had had some experience and success speaking to mountain's. They were removed by activating my faith in believing exactly what the Word of God said for me to do, after all I can read and follow instructions.

I believed I received and God honored His Word. When thoughts of doubt would come into my mind I would cast them down according to 2 Corinthians 10:4-5, casting down imaginations and every high thing that exalts itself against the knowledge of God. The knowledge of God is the Word of God and all the promises of God are yes and amen.

You would need to find a promise in the Word and what the Word of God says about your situation; your mountain. The Holy Spirit is the teacher and He will guide you into all truth. In my situation I already knew what promise I would stand on, and it was Mark 11:23-24 and I knew that I could not allow doubt to enter into my heart and mind. You cannot let doubt rule your thought life.

When you are speaking to mountains you must have a single mind full of faith. Faith is your substance, and your faith is your answer. Faith speaks the desire, and remember what this scriptures say, "Whatsoever you desire when you pray believe you receive and you shall have it." Believing is your part and the "you shall have it" is God's part. You must state in no uncertain terms what you are believing God for, and you must have a scripture to back your prayer up.

The Word of heaven is behind you. Faith pleases God and with strong faith, God will surely answer your prayer of believing faith, and God will become the rewarder of your faith because you are diligently seeking God by faith to bring your answer. Real faith has the answer before it sees the evidence manifested in the natural realm, because with in your mouth your faith reaches into the heavenly realms, and God's Word will bring the omnipotent God on the scene on your behalf.

God loves you and He will move heaven and earth for His children of faith. Your faith will set in motion all of Heaven to move on your behalf, so that you can get exactly what you have faith for. As long as you limit God and His promises, you shall have limited results. I refused to limit my believing or taking off any limits with God's Word so I can walk in the realm of the all-powerful mountain moving Word of God. For God's Word takes a man into the supernatural bringing forth fruit, and this is prayer fruit unto God.

I was to speak to this indictment and God would answer accordingly to His Word and my believing, and bring Mark11:22-23 to pass in evidence. My faith was my substance. My faith was my answer.

Hebrews 11:1 (KJV)
1 Now faith is the substance of things hoped for, the evidence of things not seen.

Hebrews 11:6 (KJV)
6 But without faith it is impossible to please him: for he that cometh to God must believe that he is, and that he is a rewarder of them that diligently seek him.

2 Corinthians 10:4-5 (KJV)
4 (For the weapons of our warfare are not carnal, but mighty through God to the pulling down of strong holds;)
5 Casting down imaginations, and every high thing that exalted itself against the knowledge of God, and bringing into captivity every thought to the obedience of Christ;

The weapons of our warfare are not carnal, and they are not of this world, but are mighty, divinely powerful weapon's filled with God's ability to overthrow fortresses and high systems of thoughts that exalt themselves against the knowledge of God, which is the Word of God, and according to His divine power at work within us, so that we have everything for life and Godliness.

We can overthrow these imaginations and reasoning's that rise against the knowledge God and the knowledge of God is His Word. We cast these imaginations down by His divine power supplied through the new nature; the divine nature. We live in the realm of heavenly thoughts for through the Word, we begin to think like Heaven and we act like citizens of Heaven. We are people of the Word and if the Bible says it that settles it for us.

The Word causes us to have the mind of heaven because the mind of Christ belongs unto us. The mind of Christ is a mind full of faith just like Jesus had. We have the same Holy Spirit, for our human spirit has been regenerated and renewed by the Holy Spirit. We are God's own workmanship created in Christ Jesus unto good works, which God has ordained us to walk in, or conduct our life by.

This brings us back to Mark 11:23-24 Jesus said not to doubt in your heart because the hidden man of the heart is your regenerated human spirit. Notice that Jesus did not mention the thoughts of your head. Your head is your mind and will receive many thoughts that are not the thoughts of your spirit. You have authority over these thoughts that oppose the Word of God, so do not obey all the thoughts that come into your mind. Only obey the thoughts that line up with the Word of God.

The natural man receives not the things which are of the Spirit of God. Our earth suit, or our body we received by being born into this world. This earth suit was given to us from the first Adam, and we are stuck in it until we believers get our new one at the resurrection.

Our spirit man is already born from above by us accepting Jesus Christ as our Lord and Savior. We are renewing our minds with His WORD (for the weapons of our warfare are not carnal, but mighty through God to the pulling down of strongholds). We are in a war with the evil spirits, for we wrestle not against flesh and blood, but against principalities, against powers, against the rulers of the darkness of this world, against spiritual wickedness in high places.

The evil thoughts they place in your mind are thoughts relating to the old man, your old way of living, and they must be eradicated and replace with the new ones. We act on the Word of God according to a promise which we are believing to receive, and God will bring that to pass. The word of God will not return to Him void of power, but it shall accomplish that which He pleases and that is to see your victory over your mountain.

Ephesians 2:10 (KJV)
10 For we are his workmanship, created in Christ Jesus unto good works, which God hath before ordained that we should walk in them.

You are ordained to walk in the victory of Jesus with the Words of our instruction manual the Bible. We are His workmanship and that means we are a work of God, the new creation man born from above. We are in Christ and our new life is created in Him. God's workmanship cannot fail when you rise up with the Word of God on your lips using your weapons, which begins with the sword of the spirit; the Word of God.

God the Holy Spirit lives inside of the new creation man and we are acting on the Words of Jesus and speaking to our mountains, "Be removed and cast into the sea," in Jesus name. The Holy Spirit is there to give you victory in any situation that arises in your life. You may not have ever tried speaking to your mountains before reading this teaching, which God has given me to impart for you to understand. One thing is for sure Jesus Words will not fall into the ground of your heart without bearing fruit for the Kingdom.

You are a believer and a believer believes the Word planted in their hearts. For out of the abundance of your heart your mouth will speak! My mouth was full of victory because my mouth is full of His Word promises. This is the way God would like you to share in that victory He has given to us in Christ Jesus. Victory comes through the Word! You have a promise, and you have your victory. Faith is believing and taking God by His word.

1 John 5:4 (KJV)
4 For whatsoever is born of God overcometh the world: and this is the victory that overcometh the world, even our faith.

We are born of God and we belong to Heaven, and the Holy Spirit will give you the power to overcome the world and anything that the world system throws against you. I am telling you right now if you will let mountain moving faith rise up inside of you, you will overcome your mountains and receive the victory that God gives through the power of His Spirit. You have overcome the world and your mountain through your faith. Jesus said "Be it unto you according to your faith" Jesus can see your faith by the words that are coming out of your mouth.

The seed of mountain moving faith arises in your heart and you say to your mountain, "Be removed and cast into the sea." My mountain was the indictments in Atlanta Fulton County Georgia. You might say that you shouldn't put yourself in a situation to be indicted, and you would be right in thinking that. I should have walked away from the crazy thoughts of my head that day but I did not, and I was caught and arrested and indicted, but God who is rich in mercy and grace accepted me turning to Him as the Supreme Authority of my life.

My God was waiting for me just as the story of the prodigal son coming home with his need, and full of guilt and shame. My Father ran to meet me putting a ring on my finger and a new robe upon my back, and welcomed me home by the cleansing power of the blood of Christ, and I was forgiven and cleansed from sin with all its guilt and shame. God meets me at my need all because of His mercy and grace. Oh, how great is the love of the Father poured out on us through Christ Jesus.

Habakkuk 2:2-3 (KJV)
2 And the LORD answered me, and said, Write
the vision, and make it plain upon tables, that
he may run that readeth it. 3 For the vision is
yet for an appointed time, but at the end it shall
speak, and not lie: though it tarry, wait for it;
because it will surely come, it will not tarry.

Now I am going to tell you of a spiritual principle that I learned many years ago. I am going to tell you exactly how and what I did to receive the victory that overcomes the world. I wrote down my mountain moving vision so I could run to read it and speak it out loud. I wrote this petition out in a book with blank pages in a journal so I could run to read it and speak it. Who am I speaking to? I am speaking to mountain's, so I can hear myself saying, "Be removed and cast into the sea". God told me in this scripture that I would see the victory. My desire is the appointed time for victory. The victory shall come and will not tarry. The Lord will answer according to His Word to the man or woman with faith.

We have God's Word written for us to read and learn because this is God's vision; this is God's plan for his creation. All written in His Word for man's knowledge. We need to write our vision and petition down with our words which is our request to God and we need God's Word backing up what we are asking of Him. In this case I am still teaching you how I made this petition of speaking to mountains.

Philippians 4:6-7 (KJV)
6 Be careful for nothing; but in everything by prayer and supplication with thanksgiving let your requests be made known unto God. 7 And the peace of God, which passeth all understanding, shall keep your hearts and minds through Christ Jesus.

These scriptures say to us, do not be anxious about anything, but by prayer and earnest pleading together with thanksgiving let your request be known before God. KJV says, "let your request be known unto God." The Holy Spirit gave me Philippians 4:6-7 and Isaiah 54:17 for a Rhema Word, including to speak to my mountain, and as I was praying for His wisdom these scriptures came up in my spirit as Words to speak to my situation along with Mark 11:23-24.

Isaiah 54:17 (KJV)
17 No weapon that is formed against thee shall prosper; and every tongue that shall rise against thee in judgment thou shalt condemn. This is the heritage of the servants of the LORD, and their righteousness is of me, saith the LORD.

Let's look at what an indictment is? It's a written judgment that is called a true bill, which became an indictment or it could be a law suit or anything coming against you which needs removing out of your life. God has given us power to speak His Word over any situation and our faith will remove it.

Jesus said for you to speak to your mountains. You do the believing and saying, and God will bring it to pass. God watches your faith for faith has action. You do the speaking of His Word and God will perform the Word for you.

Now let's look at this scripture from the prophet Isaiah. He said by the Word of the Lord, "No weapon that is formed against you shall prosper." Since we are children of light this means that no weapon of words spoken from darkness can overcome you. The words of darkness cannot overcome the power of the light of the Word on the inside of you for it cannot prosper against you. Now every tongue spoken or written down or spoken out of darkness that rises against you, you will condemn those words spoken in darkness with the Word of God's promises. You can speak to your mountains with the light of the Word. The light from the Word will cause all darkness to flee from you.

What you have done is taken the living Word of God and you have placed a sentence upon what you are speaking against; you have condemned it. This is your heritage or now that we are born again men and woman of God, this is our inheritance as sons and daughters of the new covenant in Christ Jesus, and God has given each one of us His imparted righteousness. God has done this for us because we couldn't do it ourselves; it's God's plan and it is God's doing. God has given us the abundance of grace and the gift of righteousness to rule and reign in life through the one man Jesus Christ.

Romans 5:17 (KJV)
17 For if by one man's offence death reigned by one; much more they which receive abundance of grace and of the gift of righteousness shall reign in life by one, Jesus Christ.)

2 Corinthians 5:21 (KJV)
21 For he hath made him to be sin for us, who knew no sin; that we might be made the righteousness of God in him.

God has given us the abundance of grace and the gift of righteousness to rule in life through One Man Jesus Christ. God made Jesus Christ sin for us, but Jesus Himself knew no sin, that we might be made the righteousness of God in Him. God has placed each believer in Christ and we are identified with Christ for God made Christ the Head of the Church, the Savior of the Body of Christ, and what Jesus Christ did was for all for us. We are His purchased possession.

Now your faith moves God to manifest in your specific situation. Jesus Christ paid the price for our freedom so now use the promises of God to walk in the fullness of that freedom through the blood of Jesus Christ. We have been reconciled to God.

1 Peter 2:24 (KJV)
24 Who his own self bare our sins in his own body on the tree, that we, being dead to sins, should live unto righteousness: by whose stripes ye were healed.

2 Corinthians 5:17-18 (KJV)
17 Therefore if any man be in Christ, he is a
new creature: old things are passed away;
behold, all things are become new. 18 And all
things are of God, who hath reconciled us to
himself by Jesus Christ, and hath given to us
the ministry of reconciliation;

Chapter Seventeen
Wisdom From Above: Old Creation Vs. New Creation

2 Corinthians 5:17 (KJV)
17 Therefore if any man be in Christ, he is a
new creature: old things are passed away;
behold, all things are become new.

When a man or woman accepts the work of the cross with the redemption power of the death, burial and resurrection of Jesus Christ, that person is taken out of the old creation and placed in Christ into a new creation that God has provided for all who will receive this grace and mercy by faith. In Christ we are created into this new life for we are God's own workmanship created in Christ Jesus.

Ephesians 2:8-10 (KJV)
8 For by grace are ye saved through faith; and
that not of yourselves: it is the gift of God:
9 Not of works, lest any man should boast.
10 For we are his workmanship, created in
Christ Jesus unto good works, which God hath
before ordained that we should walk in them.

We are changed from the old creation of the

first man Adam, into the new creation created by God Himself, "In Christ" we have become changed into the image of the last Adam our Lord and Savior Jesus Christ.

1 Corinthians 15:45 (KJV)
45 And so it is written, The first man Adam was made a living soul; the last Adam was made a quickening spirit. (Quickening means a living spirit.)

The old creation has passed away from the first Adam into the new creation created by God so in Christ we have become a living spirit "in Christ," and are changed by the last Adam, our Lord and Savior Jesus Christ. Our spirits were dead because of the first Adam's sin and now because God sent Jesus Christ the last Adam, the new creation has come, and a new beginning has become available to those who will believe and receive Jesus as Lord and Savior. It is called redemption, and the blood of Jesus purchased this wonderful salvation plan for us all, and anyone who will accept and believe God's salvation promise by faith.

Jesus Christ was the beginning of this new creation, as the old has passed away and the new has come. Will you pray the salvation prayer below and receive Jesus Christ as your Lord and Savior, and thereby become a part of God's family through the finished work of the cross. You will secure your place given freely by God to enter the eternal kingdom of Jesus Christ and receive eternal life.

Romans 10:9-11 (KJV)
9 That if thou shalt confess with thy mouth the Lord Jesus, and shalt believe in thine heart that God hath raised him from the dead, thou shalt be saved. 10 For with the heart man believeth unto righteousness; and with the mouth confession is made unto salvation. 11 For the scripture saith, Whosoever believeth on him shall not be ashamed.

Salvation Prayer
Heavenly Father in Jesus name I ask according to your WORD that says…Whosoever shall call upon the name of the Lord shall be saved. (Acts 2:21) So I lift up my voice to you and say, JESUS come into my life today and be my LORD and SAVIOR, and forgive me of all my sins. I confess with my mouth that JESUS is now my LORD and SAVIOR and I believe in my heart that God raised Him (JESUS) from the dead that I might have eternal life. Therefore your WORD says that I am saved

right now.

Then according to Luke 11:13 your Word says, "How much more shall the Heavenly Father give the Holy Spirit to them that ask." So Lord I am asking you to fill me with your Holy Spirit, in Jesus Name!

Thank you HEAVENLY FATHER that my name is now written in the Book of Life, in Jesus name, Amen.

Titus 3:3-8 (KJV)
3 For we ourselves also were sometimes foolish, disobedient, deceived, serving divers lusts and pleasures, living in malice and envy, hateful, and hating one another. 4. But after that the kindness and love of God our Saviour toward man appeared, 5 Not by works of righteousness which we have done, but according to His mercy he saved us, by the washing of regeneration, and renewing of the Holy Ghost; 6 Which He shed on us abundantly through Jesus Christ our Saviour; 7 That being justified by his grace, we should be made heirs according to the hope of eternal life. 8 This is a faithful saying, and these things I will that thou affirm constantly, that they which have believed in God might be careful to

maintain good works. These things are good and profitable unto men.

Bear Fruit Ministries International
PO Box 156, Bartow Georgia 30413
Email: bearfruit@yahoo.com

Gospel track Bear Fruit Idea's

Chapter Eighteen
Confessing God's Word by Decree

Job 22:28 (KJV)
28 Thou shalt also decree a thing, and it shall be established unto thee: and the light shall shine upon thy ways.

Acts 20:32 (KJV)
32 And now, brethren, I commend you to God, and to the word of his grace, which is able to build you up, and to give you an inheritance among all them which are sanctified.

Colossians 1:9 (KJV)
9 For this cause we also, since the day we heard it, do not cease to pray for you, and to desire that ye might be filled with the knowledge of his will in all wisdom and spiritual understanding;

Colossians 1:12 (KJV)
12 Giving thanks unto the Father, which hath made us meet (qualified) to be partakers of the inheritance of the saints in light:

John 15:7 (KJV)
7 If ye abide in me, and my words abide in

you, ye shall ask what ye will, and it shall be done unto you.

I decree and declare God's words over my life, and it shall be established unto me and the light shall shine upon my ways. I am God's new creation created in Christ Jesus and God Himself through the Word of His grace is building me up and gives me my inheritance among the sanctified, and God Himself builds the living Word into my spirit.

God is taking the things revealed in His Word and the Spirit of God is building those Words into me, so that I might be filled with the knowledge of His will in all spiritual wisdom and spiritual understanding, and so that the exact knowledge of my inheritance through the living Word of His power is flowing into me.

He is bringing forth all that the living Christ is to me, and Christ is being formed in me. Christ is the vine life flowing into me and I am a living branch producing fruit unto God. The Spirit of Christ lives in me and I am giving thanks unto the Father who has given me the ability to enjoy my share of the inheritance of the saints in light. I am qualified by my Father to be a partaker of all the ability of the divine nature and to enjoy all that the blood of Christ purchased for me through the Eternal Spirit, so now I can walk in the light and the glory of it all. In Jesus Name, Amen!

About the Author

Newman Smith's life story of the Grace of God is a Story of the Power of Redemption. He was born as a man of pure heart, challenged by the devil and through life changing experiences of everyday challenges and prison time, was brought back into the arms of God by faith in Jesus Christ.

God is now using him in Holy Spirit directed ministry to the incarcerated, and those he comes in contact with to help them find deliverance and the peace of Jesus in their hearts.

Colossians 1:12-14 (KJV)

Contact information

Newman C. Smith Jr
PO Box 156
Bartow, Georgia 30413

Email: **thevictorywalker@gmail.com**

Link to Newman Smiths Testimony

https://www.youtube.com/watch?v=gty_YD b5Sb4

Made in the USA
Columbia, SC
20 June 2022

61937163R00111